MYANMAR
PHRASE
BOOK

MYANMAR PHRASE BOOK

A Quick and Effective Way to Learn Myanmar Conversation

Ma Tin Cho Mar @
Noorjahan Bi Bi

Pelanduk
Publications

Published by
Pelanduk Publications (M) Sdn. Bhd.
(Co. No: 113307-W)
12 Jalan SS13/3E, Subang Jaya Industrial Estate,
47500 Subang Jaya, Selangor, Malaysia.
e-mail: *rusaone@tm.net.my*
website: *www.pelanduk.com*

Perpustakaan Negara Malaysia   Cataloguing-in-Publication Data

Ma Tin Cho Mar @ Noorjahan Bi Bi
    Myanmar phrase book : a quick and effective way to learn Myanmar
    conversation / Ma Tin Cho Mar.
    Bibliography: p. 195
    ISBN 978-967-978-976-8
    1. Burmese language—Conversation and phrase books.
    2. Burmese language—Spoken Burmese. 3. Burmese language—Textbooks
    for foreign speakers—English. I. Title.
    495.883421

Printed and bound in Malaysia.

Contents

Preface

It is said that a native speaker is the only good source of first hand knowledge of the pronunciation and usage of any language. But in situations where native speaker is not available, books like this one come in handy.

This book has been compiled throughout the years while teaching Myanmar Language in the University of Malaya, choosing an effective approach so as to make teaching more interesting and learning more enjoyable without any difficulty.

The words and phrases used in this book are confined to the basic colloquial forms which can be used while conversing with the people of Myanmar or when dealing with situations likely to be encountered at the immigration, hotels, restaurants, renting taxis, sightseeing, money changers, shopping and so on.

I sincerely hope that the students will find this book useful and practice its contents to improve their skill in speaking the Myanmar language.

Ma Tin Cho Mar @ Noorjahan Bi Bi

MYANMAR IN BRIEF

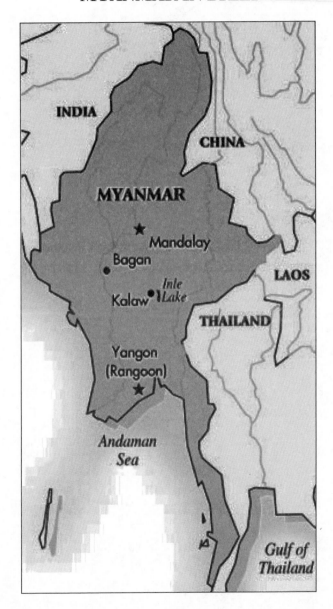

The Nation

Myanmar history trace back to the early 11th Century when King Anawrahta united the country and organized the First Myanmar Empire in Bagan more than 20 years before the Norman Conquest of England in 1066. The Bagan Empire covers the areas of the present day Myanmar and the entire Menam Valley in Thailand and lasted two centuries. The Second Myanmar Empire was founded in mid 16th Century by King Bayinnaung. King Alaungpaya founded the last Myanmar Dynasty in 1752 and it was during the zenith of this Empire that British shifted into Myanmar. Similar to India, Myanmar became a British colony but only after three Anglo-Myanmar Wars in 1825, 1852 and 1885. During the Second World War, Myanmar was occupied by the Japanese from 1942 till the return of the Allied Forces in 1945. Myanmar has become a sovereign independent state since 4th January 1948 after 62 years under the colonial administration. It is notable to point that Myanmar is the country that regained her independence first though she was the last country occupied by the British in the Southeast Asian region.

Myanmar is the biggest country in mainland Southeast Asia and borders on China, Laos, Thailand, Bangladesh and India, having long coastlines with the Andaman Sea and the Bay of Bengal. These prominent locations could well lead Myanmar to become the regional economic leader and centre for Southeast Asia. Formerly known as Burma, Myanmar has an area of 676,577 sq km. The largest city in Myanmar is Yangon (formerly known as Rangoon) with a population of over four million people. Yangon, formerly being Myanmar's capital, is considered to be the heart and core of Myanmar.

People

The Republic of the Union of Myanmar is made up of 135 national races: speaking over one hundred languages and dialects (ref: *http://*

en.wikipedia.org/wiki/Burma). The name of Myanmar holds all nationalities. The major races are the Kachin, Kayah, Kayin, Chin, Bamar, Mon, Rakhine and Shan. There are 7 states and 7 divisions in Myanmar.

Religion

Over 80% of the Myanmar are Buddhists. There are also Christians, Muslims, Hindus and even some animists. Most Myanmar are Buddhist of the Theravada stream. Buddhism here comes with a heavy dosage of bamahsan chinn. Buddhism influenced complex word describing the gentle personality of many, which includes undying respect for elders, modesty in dressing and a preference for subtlety rather than loudness or directness. Central to their religious beliefs is karma, the concept that good begets good and evil begets evil. Another belief is that all living things go through reincarnation. If a person has committed sins, he or she will be reincarnated into a lower level being such as an animal or suffered in Hell; on the other hand, if he has done good deeds, he will be elevated to a higher level of existence to the world of devas. The ultimate aim in life according to Buddhist belief is to escape the cycle of rebirth and reach Nirvana. There are also Nats or the Spiritual beings worship in Myanmar. They are believed to be extremely powerful beings for helping people.

Superstitions

A few of Myanmar people, especially those from the rural areas, believe in superstitions. Astrology, palmistry and clairvoyance are sometimes relied upon to make important decisions. These may include marriage, going into a business partnership, naming a baby and others. To offset bad luck, certain meritorious deeds or

Yadaya may be performed such as setting free some live birds or animals, building a footbridge or mending a road.

Superstition of different cultures are interesting in some ways. Here are some:

- Don't go underneath a staircase. You will loose your will power.
- Don't go under a pole or rope where women used to hang-dry their lingeries. You will loose your will power.
- Don't leave a shoe or slipper upside-down. It will cause bad luck.
- Don't keep a broken glass or mirror in homes. Replace the window panes as soon as possible if broken.
- Don't wash your hair within a week after a funeral in the neighborhood.
- Don't hit the pot with a ladle after you stir the curry. It is like hitting your parents' head.
- Don't hit two lids of pots and pans against each other. A tiger may bite you.
- Don't feed someone with the palm upward. The food might cause you disorder.
- Don't clip your nails at night. Ghosts don't like that.
- Don't take kids to dark places. Ghosts may posses them. Carrying some hairs of an elephant tail will avoid evil.

Culture

Myanmar lies on the crossroads of two of the world's great nations: China and India. Its culture is a blend of both interspersed with Myanmar native traits and characteristics. Buddhism has great influence on daily life of the Myanmar. The people have preserved the traditions of close family ties, respect for the elders, reverence for Buddhism and simple native dress. Myanmars are known for their simple hospitality and friendliness. The Myanmar people can be as proud of their country and culture as any nationality. Locals gush over about kings, *pwe* ပွဲ (festivals), *Mohingar* မုန့်ဟင်းခါး (noodles with chicken or fish) breakfasts, great temples and many others.

Myanmar Famous Mohingar

Myanmar, endless stretch of green forests, a rural community of simple people, exotic sights and exotic food to excite the inquiring palate. The schedule of a visiting traveller to Myanmar will never be completed if he or she has not tasted the ubiquitous Mohingar or Latphet (pickled tea leaves).

Mohingar is typically synonymous with Myanmar. It is an all-time favourite, from breakfast through lunch to high teatime and even stretching to supper. Mohingar is certainly Myanmar's fastfood because it can be relished instantly without much ado pleasing and tasty. Its food value is rich in protein, carbohydrates, vitamins, minerals, etc. Its recipe is also simple, easy to prepare with ingredients within the reach of every budget.

A general run-of-the-mill recipe include the following ingredients: rice noodles, fish (fresh water or marine), fish or prawn sauce, a small measure of salted fish, lemon grass, tender banana stems, ginger, garlic, pepper, onion, turmeric powder, rice flour, dahl (Indian bean) powder, dried chilli powder and cooking oil.

The method of cooking the broth differs with each region and taste of the locality. This fish broth is taken with rice noodles and only the such composition fittingly earns the name Mohingar. The rice noodles to go with Mohingar is prepared by a special process, and carry a whiff of mild fermentation. Fresh slabs of noodles are also available, which has to be sliced to cater to individual demands. Laying a Mohingar table calls for elaborate preparation. The cooked broth is put in shining aluminium or steel receptacle and placed on open fire to keep it boiling because Mohingar is served steaming hot to bring forth the correct flavour and taste. Mohingar can be taken with other accompanying side dishes to make it a feast fit for a king, for in the market economy, the customer is naturally the king. Thus on the table are spread colourful arrays of food adornments such as fried sliced gourd with tempura (a favourite with Myanmars as french fries are to the Westerners), fried onions, fried fish cakes sliced to size, sliced hard-boiled eggs, etc. Alongside with these dishes are laid a dish of dried chilli for those who like it hot, slices of fresh lemon to squeeze into the preparation for those who like the sweet-and-sour flavour, chopped green coriander leaves. All these ingredients are mixed into the piece de resistance and alors and there is none equal to this exciting delicacy of pure Myanmar origin.

Each region, each town, even each reputable shop has its own secret recipe to make it distinct to attract customers. Some add coconut milk to heighten aroma and flavour, but such preparation are frowned upon by the senior clients as it adversely tend to raise blood pressure to dizzy heights. The most common species of fresh-water fish used in Mohingar broth are carp, catfish, butterfish, etc.

The Monhingar along the coastal regions is cooked with marine fish. Deltaic towns in the numerous lakes called 'inns' meaning large expanse of water catchment where fish breed. The broth is prepared with a liberal mix of fish fresh from the latest catch. In Upper Myanmar region to the north, customers prefer thick broth and so it is an overtone of dahl flour.

Pickled Tea Leaves or Laphet

 Taking tea usually without milk and sugar is the custom in the Shan State, as it is throughout the Republic of the Union of Myanmar because everyone, young or elderly, male or female, layman or monk, drinks tea in the traditional way but rarely in a modern way mixing it with milk and sugar. Tea is served at every social or religious ceremony and function. In every household there is at least one member of the family who likes to have a cup of plain tea as soon as he or she gets up from bed. The first duty of the housewife when she gets up is to boil water and prepare a pot of tea, not only for the grandfather, grandmother, father or husband, but also for herself and her children. Guests, near or far and whoever comes for a visit is offered a cup of plain tea. It has become customary for everyone in the Shan State to present tea as gifts to visitors either in dried leaves or in pickled state.

Tea shops are crowded with people, both young and old. Holding a cup of plain tea and slowly sipping it is quite refreshing. People would also do their business at the tea shops by the roadside. Tea serves many purposes – social, economic and religious. Nobody can run away from tea. Tea has become a national drink. The chief crop of cultivation among the Palaung is tea. The tea tree or tea-shrub is indigenous and grows wild all over the hills but the cropping is closely associated with Tawngpang. Tea is abundant in places like Mong Long, Mong Mit, Mong Khe, Panglong and in Petkang areas of Keng Tung State. Tea-shrub likes a high latitude, shade and dampness. Tawngpang is the most suitable place for such conditions. The tea is made in two forms: one, Neng Yam or wet or pickled tea, and the other dry tea. One needs skills and experience for picking, drying and curing of tea leaves. The leaves are steamed in a wooden strainer with a perforated bamboo bottom which is placed over a large cauldron of boiling water. It is steamed for a few minutes just to moisten and soften the leaves so that they can be easily and quickly rolled with the fingers on a mat while another lot is being steamed. These steamed and rolled leaves are spread out on the screen resulting in dry tea. The making of the pickled variety is more complicated. The steamed leaves are heaped together in a pulp mass and thrown into baskets and left until the next day. The baskets are then put into pits in the ground and covered with heavy weights placed on top of them. Inspection is often made to see how fermentation is progressing and sometimes there is re-steaming.

The Palaungs are the only tea growers who produce the "pickled tea" and some call it "salad tea". The Palaung tea plantations are on steep hill-sides. It takes three years to get a crop, and after ten years or more the plants weaken and output will be poor. The Palaungs does not produce much tea for their own consumption and tea drinking culture amongst them could possibly elapse. Therefore, tea cultivation should be encouraged and research should be made to improve production so that good quality tea would be available not only for domestic consumption but also for the export market. Food technology should also be applied to make tea not only as a beverage but as an item of nutritious food in the future.

Much of the dry tea goes to different parts of Myanmar and some to Yunnan across the border. Pickled tea is transported down to Mandalay and Yangon for general distribution. Myanmar people like pickled tea more than anyone else and it has become a delicacy for them and is eaten mixed with a little oil, salt, garlic, asafoetida and topped off with sesame seeds.

In Myanmar culture, the people traditionally use the right hand for eating. As the left hand is used for personal hygiene, it is preferable to use the right hand when you give something to someone. At the same time, to use only one hand seems half-hearted, so to show warmth, Myanmar people sometimes use both hands when shaking hands. To show more respect when giving something to someone, it is customary to touch the right forearm with your left hand. Beckoning to a Myanmar with one finger curled up is seen as disrespectful. If you have to beckon, do so with your palm down. You do not need appointments to visit Myanmar friends at home, and do not be surprised if they call on you without any notice. Myanmar people typically turn up for enjoyable occasions half an hour early but for some, half an hour later. When visiting a Myanmar home or office, you are usually served with something to eat or drink as this is their culture. It is better to eat and drink a little, even if you do not want it. For Myanmar people, absolute refusals are bad manners.

Language

Myanmar is the lingua franca. English is broadly understood in cities like Yangon, Mandalay, Pagan and Bago, etc. There are many linguistic groups in Myanmar, but the official language is Burmese (*Myanmar* according to the government) but English is compulsory in schools and the courts operate in both Myanmar and English. All laws are printed in both languages. Most of the population speaks Burmese, even the ethnic minorities, with the education speaking English as well. There are also quite a few who speak Chinese, Shan and Karen.

History and Background of the Myanmar Language

Burmese is the official and primary language of Myanmar. It is closely related to Tibetan and distantly related to Chinese. The government uses the term *"Myanmar"* to describe the language, although most continue to refer to the language as "Burmese". Burmese or, as the people of Burma call it, *Myanmar Batha* (the language of Myanmar) is the speech of a considerable and powerful tribe, closely connected with the Tibetans which prior to A.D. 1000, over-ran the valley of the Irrawaddy River and adopted Buddhism and the alphabet of its sacred books, which were written in Pali, alphabets founded on the ancient characters of India. Burmese was one of the earliest Tibeto-Burman languages to develop a writing system. Traditionally, it is thought that Mon scribes, brought to the city of Pagan after the sack of their capital by the Burmese king Anawrahta in A.D. 1057, provided the stimulus for adapting the Mon script to the writing of Burmese. It is likely that Mon monks, brought to Pagan Empire, after defeating the Mons, assisted in adapting their script to the writing of Burmese (Julian K. Wheatly, 1978-1979). Therefore, the Mons were initially the donor of the language and the source of the Theravada, one of the varieties of Buddhism which has flourished as the main religion of the people of Burma since that period. The earliest specimens of Burmese writing appear early in the next century and the best known of these is *Myazedi* stone manuscript in Pagan; it is also known as the *Yazar Komer* manuscript after the person who had it repaired. Dated A.D. 1112, it is in four languages: Pali, Mon, Pyu and Burmese. There have been some changes since the inscriptional period, most notably: Consistent use of the "rounded" rather than the "square" style of letters, changes in permissible combinations of vowels and final consonant signs, and stabilization of the system for marking tones (*Burmese Writing*, Julian K. Wheatley, 1978-1979 and *English Borrowings in the Burmese Language*, Hasmat Bi@ Noreen Rashid, 2009).

Burma is a multi-national state which has a population of around 58 million. About two thirds of its population is Burmans and the other third is made up of a variety of ethnic groups, including Tibeto-Burman speaking people such as Chin, Naga and Karen. Mon-Khmer people such as the Mon, Padaung and the Shan whose language is very closely related to that of Thai and other nationalities such as Chinese and Indians. Most of the ethnic groups have their own languages and their own writing systems but they utilize their own language within their family and in daily transactions whereas in schools or dealing with authorities and in cross-cultural communications, they use the Burmese language. Therefore Burmese emerges as the language of education and the media of business and administration, and of communication between ethnic groups.

Although Burmese language is now spoken throughout the country, regional speech variations can be detected in terms of dialect, pronunciations and vocabularies. This kind of variations can only be attested in colloquial forms but not in written forms. For writing, the standard Burmese is used.

The sound system of Burmese comprises thirty-three consonants (of which twenty-nine are usable, but the whole is put into requisition for words borrowed from Pali), nine vowels, three diphthongs and four tones. There are no articles, no inflection of the verb to agree with tenses or numbers nor declension of nouns and pronouns according to gender, number or case. The distinctive Burmese Alphabet consists almost entirely of circles or portions of circles used in various combinations. It evolved at a time when writing was generally written on palm leaves, the letters traced by means of stylus. Thus straight lines were impossible because they would cause to split.

Pronunciation Differences

Burmese is a **tonal** language, consisting of four tones (low, high, creaky, checked). All dialects of Burmese in Myanmar adhere to this rule, although vocabulary usage varies from region to region. Despite its Upper Burmese origins, the standard dialect of Burmese today comes from Yangon (Lower Burma), because of the largest city's media influence. It used to be that the speech from Mandalay (Upper Burma) represented standard Burmese. Most of the differences between Upper and Lower Burmese are in vocabulary usage, not in the accent or pronunciation. For example, the most noticeable feature of the Mandalay dialect is its use of the first person pronoun ကျွန်တော် (*kya.nau*) for both males and females, whereas in Yangon, ကျွန်မ (*kya.ma.*) is used by females.

As mentioned earlier, the wrong usage of tones will send a wrong message. For example: when using these three words... မေ *may* (mother) မေ့ *may.*(forget) မေး *may:*(ask), one has to be careful of the different tones. If a person wants to say 'I am asking you' *Kyama shin. go may: nay de`*, instead if she says: *Kyama shin. go may. nay de`* (I forget you), the sentence is sending a wrong message. Hence students must listen to the sounds of a language carefully in order for them to make tonal distinctions. To pronounce words properly, they need to hear them properly. They must know intonation patterns of the language so that people can distinguish clearly what is being said.

Minor pronunciation differences do exist within regions of Irrawaddy valley. Take the example of the pronunciation of ဆွမ်း ("food offering [to a monk]"): [sún] is preferred in Lower Burma instead of [swán], which is preferred in Upper Burma.

Burmese has a complicated set of vowels, containing 12 vowels.

Diphthongs
ai
> like the 'i' in site

au
> like the 'ou' in out; always used with a consonant ending

ei
> like the 'a' in ache

ou
> like the 'oa' in moat

Monophthongs
a
> like the 'a' in mama

13

e

    like the 'e' in she

i

    like the 'ea' in meat

o

    like the 'o' in tote

u

    like the 'ew' in lewd

ih

    like the 'i' in trip

Burmese consonants are aspirated (contains an 'h' sound) and unaspirated (does not contain an 'h' sound). Aspirated and unaspirated consonants are romanised irregularly because a uniform system does not yet exist.

b

    like the 'b' in bat

d

    like the 'd' in dagger

g

    like the 'g' in gap

h

    like the 'h' in house

k

    like the 'k' in tanker

kh

    like the 'c' in cat

ky

    like the 'j' in jeep

l

    like the 'l' in love

m

    like the 'm' in mad

n
> like the 'n' in nut

ng
> like the 'ng' in dancing

ny
> like the 'ni' in onion

p
> like the 'p' in page

ph
> like the 'p' in pig

r
> becomes a 'y', or is silent

s
> like a 's' in sing, or becomes a 'th' sound

shw
> like the 'sh' in shack

hs
> like a 's' in sound

t
> like a 't' in that

th
> like a 't' in tongue

w
> like a 'w' in win

y
> like a 'y' in young

z
> like a 'z' in zoo

For the examples that follow, transliterations are given in a slightly modified version of the standard Blagden-Duroiselle system (summarized by Okell 1971).

Table 1 shows the 33 consonant signs of Burmese arranged in traditionally order (reading from left to right).

Table 1: Consonants

	Voiceless Stops		Voiced Stops		Nasals
	Unaspirated	*Aspirated*	*Unaspirated*	*Aspirated*	
Velar	က k [k]	ခ kh [k]	ဂ g [g]	ဃ gh [g]	င n [n]
Palatal	စ c [s]	ဆ ch [s]	ဇ j [z]	ဈ jh [z]	ည mn [n] ဉ n [n]
Retroflex	ဋ t [t]	ဌ th [t]	ဍ d [d]	ဎ dh [d]	ဏ n [n]
Dental	တ t [t]	ထ th [t]	ဒ d [d]	ဓ dh [d]	န n [n]
Labial	ပ p [p]	ဖ ph [p]	ဗ b [b]	ဘ bh [b]	မ m [m]
Sonorants					
	ယ y [j]	ရ r [j]	လ l [l]	ဝ w [w]	သ s [ ]
		ဟ h [h]	ဠ l [l]	အ o [?]	

Source: Information were obtained from thesis: Hasmat Bi @ Noreen Rashid (2009), *English Borrowings in the Burmese Language.*

Table 2 shows the main vowel and tone combinations in open syllables; all diacritics vowels are given with the vowel support sign (pronounced [?]). A tall version of the sign ‑ာ a is used when the combinations of consonant and vowel would be confused with other consonants; thus ပ p + ‑ာ a is written ပါ pa [pa] to avoid confusion with ပာ h.

Table 2: Vowels and Tones (Open Syllables)

	Front Vowels	Central Vowels	Back Vowels
Tone	*Initial Diacritic*	*Initial Diacritic*	*Initial Diacritic*
Primary Vowels			
Creaky	ဣ ◌ိ အိ I [I]	အ – a [a']	ဥ ◌ု အု u [u']
Low	ဤ ◌ီ အီ I [I]	–ာ အာ a [a]	ဦ ◌ူ အူ u [u]
High	◌ိ: အိ:	–ား အား: a [a]	ဦး ◌ူး: u [u]
Mid Vowels			
High Low	ဧ ေ– ေအ e [e]	◌ို အို ui [o]
High	ေ–း ေအး e [è]	◌ိုး အိုး: ui: [o]
Creaky	ေ–. ေအ. e [e]	◌ို. အို. ui. [o]
Low	–ယ် အယ် ay [ ]	ေသာ် ေ–ာ် ေအာ် o [ ]
High	◌ဲ အဲ ai [ ]	ဩ ေ–ာ ေအာ o [ ]
Creaky	◌ဲ. အဲ ai. [ ]	ေ–ာ. ေအာ. o [ ]

Source: Information were obtained from thesis: Hasmat Bi @ Noreen Rashid (2009), *English Borrowings in the Burmese Language*.

Consonants written without a vowel sign contain an inherent vowel: မ ma, လ la. However, the vowel may be cancelled by a "killer stroke" over the consonant; thus မ် is syllable-final *m*. Other vowels are indicated with diacritics according to Table 2: မိ *mi*, မု *mu*, မေ *me*, မာ *ma*, မော *mo* [mɔ̀], မို *mui* [mo], etc. The vowel signs also contain inherent tones.

The following shows how Burmese (Myanmar) vowels combined with consonants and got resonance.

Burmese (Myanmar) Vowels to be Combined with Consonants

LEVEL I

1. *yaycha & yaycha wisahnitlonepuk*

–	– ာ	– ား
–	– ါ	– ါး
အ	အာ	အား
a.	a	a:

2. *lonegyitin, lonegyitin sankha & lonegyitin sankha*
   wisahnitlonepuk

ိ	ီ	ီး
အိ	အီ	အီး
ဣ	ဤ	
i.	i	i:

3. *tiqchaungngyn, hnitchaung ngyn & hnitchaungngyn*
   wisahnitlonepuk

ု	ူ	ူး
အု	အူ	အူး
ဥ	ဦ	ဦး
u	ue	ue:

4. *thawaihtoe, thawaihtoe aukamyint & thawaihtoe*
   wisahnitlonepuk

ေ–	ေ–ႉ	ေ–း
ေအ	ေအႉ	ေအး
ay	ayt	aye:

၈	၍
a	yak

5. *yathat, naukpyik aukamyint & naukpyik*

–ယ်	ႆ	ႆ
အယ်	အဲ့	အဲ
e'	e'.	e`

yathat aukamyint

–ယ်ႉ
အယ်ႉ
e'.

6. *thawaihtoe yaycha, thawaihtoe yaycha aukamyint &*
   thawaihtoe yaychashaihtoe (yaychathat)

ေ–ာ	ေ–ာႉ	ေ–ာ်
ေအာ	ေအာႉ	ေအာ်
aw	ort	or

ေသာ်	or
သ	aw

7. *nathat, nathat aukmyint & nathat wisahnitlonepuk*

–န်	–န်ႉ	–န်း
အန်	အန်ႉ	အန်း
an	ant	ann

19

–မ်   –မ့်   –မ်း
အမ်   အမ့်   အမ်း
am   amt   am:

အမ့်   အမ့်.

8. *yaypint & yayit*

ကျ   ကျာ   ကျား   ပြ   ပြာ   ပြား
kya   kyar   kyar: pya   pyar   pyar:

9. *waswe & waswe yaycha & waswe yaycha wisahnitlonepuk*

ကွ   ကွာ   ကွား
kwa   kwar   kwar:

10. *thawaihtoe yaypint waswe & yayit waswe*

ကျွေး   ကျွဲ   ကျွ   ကျွာ   ကျွား
kywaye kywe`   kywa   kywar   kywar:

11. *hahtoe, hathtoe yaycha & hahtoe yaycha wisahnitlonepuk,*
    hahtoe lonegyitin

 င   ငာ   ငါး   ရှိ
hnga   hngar   hngar: she

12. *yaypint hahtoe & yayit hahtoe*

 မျှ   မျှား   လျှ   မြှေး
hmya   hmyar: hlar   hmyae:

13. waswe hahtoe

	ဝ̄		
လွ	လွာ	လွား	့နွေ`
hlwa	hlwar	hlwar:	hnwe`

14. tiqchaungngyn lone gyitin, tiqchaungngyn lonegyitin
   aukamyint & tiqchaungngyn lonegyitin wisahnitlonepuk

္	္	္
ို	ို့	ို:
	္ယဲ့	
ကို	ကို့	ကို:
ko	koe.	koe:

LEVEL II

1.   ngathat, ngathat aukamyint & ngathat wisahnitlonepuk

–င်	–င့်	–င်:
အင်	အင့်	အင်:
in	int.	ann:

–ၟ်	–ၟ့်	–ၟ်:
အၟ်	အၟ့်	အၟ်:
in	int.	ann:

2.   thawaihtoe yaycha ngathat, thawaihtoe yaycha ngathat
   aukamyint & thawai htoe yaycha ngathat wisahnitlonepuk

ေ–ာင်	ေ–ာင့်	ေ–ာင်:
အောင်	အောင့်	အောင်:
aun	aunt.	aunn:

3. *lonegyitin tiqchaungngyn ngathat, lonegyitin tiqchaungngyn ngathat aukamyint & lonegyitin tiqchaungngyn ngathat wisahnitlonepuk*

ဣင်	ဣင့်	ဣင်း
အိင်	အိင့်	အိင်း
ain	aint.	ainn:

4. *lonegyitin nathat, lonegyitin nathat aukamyint & lonegyitin nathat wisahnitlonepuk*

ဣန်	ဣန့်	ဣန်း
အိန်	အိန့်	အိန်း
ein	eint.	einn:

ဣမ်	ဣမ့်	ဣမ်း
အိမ်	အိမ့်	အိမ်း
eim	eimt.	eim:

5. *thaythaytin tiqchaungngyn, thaythaytin tiqchaungngyn aukamyint & thaythaytin tiqchaungngyn wisahnitlonepuk*

ဤ	ဤ့	ဤး
အုံ	အုံ့	အုံး
on	ont.	onn:

tiqchaungngyn nathat, tiqchaungngyn nathat aukamyint & tiqchaungngyn nathat wisahnitlonepuk

ဤန်	ဤန့်	ဤန်း
အုန်	အုန့်	အုန်း
on	ont.	onn:

6. *waswe ngathat, waswe ngathat aukamyint & waswe ngathat*
   wisahnitlonepuk

   ဝ်ႏ်ၟ   ဝ်ႏ်ၟ.   ဝ်ႏ်ၟး
   အွန်   အွန့.   အွန်း
   un   unt.   unn:

   waswe mathat, waswe mathat aukamyint & waswe mathat
   wisahnitlonepuk

   ဝ်မ်ၟ   ဝ်မ်ၟ.   ဝ်မ်ၟး
   အွမ်   အွမ့.   အွမ်း
   um   umt.   umm:

7. *kathat*
   – က်
   အက်
   et

8. *thawaihtoe yaycha kathat*
   ၜောက်
   အောက်
   auk

9. *tiqchaungngyn lonegyitin kathat*
   ိက်
   အိုက်
   aik

10. *sathat*
    – စ်
    အစ်
    is

23

11. tathat & pathat

　　　–တ်　　–ပ်
　　　အတ်　　အပ်
　　　at

12. waswe tathat & waswe pathat

　　　ွတ်　　ွပ်
　　　အွတ်　　အွပ်
　　　ut

13. lonegyitin tathat & lonegyitin pathat

　　　ိတ်　　ိပ်
　　　အိတ်　　အိပ်
　　　eik

14. tiqchaungngyn tathat & tiqchaungngyn pathat

　　　ုတ်　　ုပ်
　　　အုတ်　　အုပ်
　　　oke

Dialect

Burma is an enormous country with a space of over 260,000 miles and it is a simmering stew of ethnic diversity where area of the Burmese majority, is encircled by separate ethnic states for the Chins, Kachins, Shans, Karens, Kayahs, Arakanese, Mons and many other minority ethnic groups. There are a number of mutually intelligible Burmese dialects in the Burmese language, with a largely uniform standard dialect used by most Burmese speakers, who live throughout the Irrawaddy River valley and more distinctive non-standard dialects that emerge as one toward peripheral areas of the country. These dialects include *Palaw*, *Beik/Myeik* (Merguese), and

Dawei (Tavoyan) in Taninthayi Division, *Yaw* in Magway Division, *Intha* and *Danu* in Shan State, *Rakhine* (Arakanese) in Rakhine State and *Marma* in Bangladesh. Despite vocabulary and pronunciation differences, there is mutual intelligibility among Burmese dialects, as for the most part, they share the same four tones, consonant clusters and the Burmese script. However, several dialects differ in Burmese with respect to vocabulary, lexical particles and rhymes.

The most obvious difference between Upper Burmese and Lower Burmese is that Upper Burmese speech still differentiates maternal and paternal sides of a family. The following table shows the difference between Upper Burmese and Lower Burmese speech of maternal and paternal sides.

Table 3: Different Dialects

Term	Upper Burmese	Lower Burmese	Myeik Dialect
• Paternal aunt (older) • Paternal aunt (younger)	• အရီးကြီး *(ayi gyi)* • အရီလေး *(ayi lay)*	• ဒေါ်ကြီး *(daw gyi)*	• မိကြီး *(mi gyi)*
• Maternal aunt (older) • Maternal aunt (younger)	• ဒေါ်ကြီး *(daw gyi)* • ဒေါ်လေး *(daw lay)*	• ဒေါ်လေး *(daw lay)*	• မိငယ် *(mi nge)*
• Paternal uncle (older) • Paternal uncle (younger)	• �‌ဘကြီး *(ba gyi)* • ဘလေး *(ba lay)*	• ဘကြီး *(ba gyi)*	• ဖကြီး *(pha gyi)*

• Maternal uncle (older) • Maternal uncle (younger)	• အရီးကြီး *(ayi gyi)* • အရီးလေး *(ayi lay)*	• ဘလေး *(ba lay)*	• ဖေဂယ် *(pha ge)*

Source: Information were obtained from the internet *http://en.wikipedia.org/wiki/Burmese_language*

The youngest (paternal or maternal) aunt may be called ဒွေးလေး *(dwe le')*, and the youngest paternal uncle ဘဒွေး *(badwe')*.

In confirmation to the power of media, the Yangon-based speech is gaining currency even in Upper Burma. Upper Burmese-specific usage, while historically and technical accurate, is increasingly viewed as countrified speech, or at best regional speech. In fact, some usages are already considered strictly regional Upper Burmese speech, and are likely dying out. For example:

Table 4: Different Dialect

Term	Upper Burmese	Standard Burmese
• Elder brother (to a male) • Elder brother (to a female)	• နောင် *(naun)* • ကို *(ko)*	• ကို *(ko)*
• Younger brother (to a male) • Younger brother (to a female)	• ညီ *(nyi)* • မောင် *(maung)*	

26

• Elder sister (to a male) • Elder sister (to a female)	• မ *(ma)*	
• Younger sister (to a male) • Younger sister (to a female)	• နှစ်မ *(hnit ma)* • ညီမ *(nyi ma)*	• ညီမ *(nyi ma)*

Source: Information were obtained from the internet *http://en.wikipedia.org/ wiki/Burmese_language*

Dialogues
Zaga A-chi-a-cha Pyaw Han
စကားအချီအချပြောဟန် ။

"Hello, Madam."
"Mingalaba Khinbya"
"Hello, Sir."
"Mingalaba Shin"

Hello.
Mingalaba.
မင်္ဂလာပါ

Hello. (*informal*)
Nei kaung la?
နေကောင်းလား

How are you?
Nei kaon la?
နေကောင်းလား

28

Fine, thank you.
Ne kaon ba de.
နေကောင်းပါတယ်

What is your name?
Kamya ye na mee ba le?
ခင်ဗျားရဲ့နာမည် ဘာလဲ

My name is ....
Kya nau na mee .... ba.
ကျွန်တော့်နာမည် .... ပါ။

Nice to meet you.
Twe ya da wanta ba de.
တွေ့ရတာဝမ်းသာဘာတယ်။

Please.
Kyeizu pyu yue.
ကျေးဇူးပြု၍

Thank you.
Kyeizu tin ba de.
ကျေးဇူးတင်ပါတယ်

You're welcome.
Ya ba de.
ရပါတယ်။

Yes.
Ho de.
ဟုတ်တယ်

No.
Ma ho bu.
မဟုတ်ဘူး။

"Please come in. Sit here."
"Di Mha Htain Bar"
"Alright."
"Hoke Ket Shin"

Excuse me. (getting attention)
Ka mya.
ခင်ဗျား

Excuse me. (begging pardon)
Khwit pyu bar.
ခွင့်ပြုပါ။

Goodbye.
Thwa dau me.
သွားတော့မယ်။

Goodbye. (informal)
Thwa dau me.
သွားတော့မယ်။

I can't speak name of language [well].
Ba ma za ga go [kaung-kaung] ma pyaw thet bu.
ဗမာစကားကို ကောင်းကောင်းမပြောတတ်ဘူး

Do you speak English?
In glei za ga go pyaw thet de la?
အင်္ဂလိပ်စကားကို ပြောတတ်သလား

Is there someone here who speaks English?
In glei za-ga pyaw thet de lu di ma shi la?
အင်္ဂလိပ်စကား ပြောတတ်တဲ့ လူရှိလား

Help!
A ku nyi lo de!
အကူအညီလိုတယ်။

Look out!
Ai ya! Kyi!
အရေးကြီး။

Good morning.
Mingalabar.
မင်္ဂလာပါ။

Good night. (to sleep)
Eigh douh meh.
အိပ်တော့မယ်။

I don't know.
Kya-nau ma thi bu.
ကျွန်တော် မသိဘူး။

I don't understand.
Kya-nau na ma ley bu.
ကျွန်တော် နားမလည်ဘူး။

Where is the toilet?
Ein da ga be ma leh khinbya?
အိမ်သာ ဘယ်မှာလဲ ခင်ဗျား။

Let's Speak a Little Bit of Burmese

Hello	*Mingalaba*
How are you?	*Nei kaun: la:*
Fine.	*Kaun: bar de`*
Thank you	*Kyei: zu: tin bar de`*
Thank you very much	*Kyei: zu: amya: gyi: tin bar de`*
Don't mention/ never mind	*Kek sa ma shi bar bu:*
Yes	*Houk ke`*
No	*Ma houk phu:*
Okay. All right	*Kaun: bi*
Excuse me	*Kwint pyu bar*
Sorry	*Seik mashi. bar ne*
How much?	*Bei lauk le:*
Welcome	*Kyo zo bar de`*
Have you eaten?	*Sar: pyi bi la:*
Have eaten	*Sar: pyi bi*
Haven't eaten	*Ma sar te' bu:*
Understand?	*Nar: le` da la:*
I understand.	*Nar: le` de`*
I don't understand.	*Nar: ma le` bu:*
Don't know	*Ma thi bu*
Glad to meet you.	*Twei yada wun tha bar de`*
See you again	*Nauk twei da pau*
Goodbye	*Thwa bar ohn mei*

The Alphabets and Pronunciations

The Burmese or Myanmar script developed from the Mon script, which was adapted from a southern Indian script during the 8th century. The earliest known inscriptions in the Burmese script date from the 11th century. Following are the notable features:

- Type of writing system: syllabic alphabet – each letter has an inherent vowel [a]. Other vowels sounds are indicated using separate letters or diacritics which appear above, below, in front of, after or around the consonant.
- The rounded appearance of letters is a result of the use of palm leaves as the traditional writing material. Straight lines would have torn the leaves. The Burmese name for the script is *ca-lonh* 'round script'.
- Burmese is a tonal language with three main tones (high, low and creaky) and two other tones (stopped and reduced). The tones are indicated in writing using diacritics or special letters.
- **Burmese/Myanmar,** a member of the Burmese-Lolo group of the Sino-Tibetan language spoken by about 30 million people in Burma (Myanmar).

The **Karen** languages, a group of languages which are related to Burma and which are spoken by around 4 million people in Burma and Thailand.

Mon, a member of the Mon-Khmer group of the Austroasiatic languages spoken by something like 200,000 people in Burma and Thailand.

Information were obtained from the internet *http://www.omniglot.com/writing/burmese.htm*

Burmese Script

မြန်မာစာ

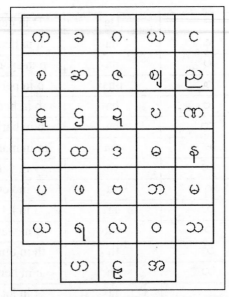

Burmese Characters	Romanized Form	Pronounced as	Vowels
က	k	*k* in kite	a:
ခ	kh	k in kate	i:
ဂ	g	g in gate	u:
ဃ	g	g in gate	ei:
င	ng	ng in ring	ou:
စ	sa	s in sink	e:
ဆ	hsa	s in see	o:
ဇ	za	z in zinc	ai:
ဈ	za	z in zebra	au:
ည	ny	ny in banyan	
ဏ	na	na in banana	
တ	ta	t in ten	
ထ	hta	t in tier	
ဒ	da	d in deer	

၁	Da	D in den	
န	na	n in near	
ပ	pa	p in spark	
ဖ	pha	p in park	
ဗ	ba	b in bed	
ဘ	ba	b in bark	
မ	ma	m in mark	
ယ	ya	y in yet	
ရ	ya	y in yet	
လ	la	l in let	
ဝ	wa	w in way	
သ	th	th in thin	
ဟ	ha	h in hen	
ဠ	la	l in let	
အ	a	a in father	

Zingala Nat is a Burmanized version of the Indian God Jangala, "The Recorder". He is traditionally represented, as here, holding a pen and a parabaik.

36

Burmese Buddhist Palm Leaf Manuscript (Kammavaca)

Parabaiks are used to record astrological and religious writings. The parabaiks are a rich source material on costumes, architecture, social and religious life of Myanmar.

Palm leaves have been the most popular writing material in India and Southeast Asia countries where Buddhism and Indian culture spread. Varying temperatures, humidity and insect destruction have not allowed the survival of early manuscripts. The earliest known surviving palm-leaf is from the 10th century. Large collections of palm-leaf manuscripts can be found in South and Southeast Asia. Most of the collections are in monasteries, libraries and historical institutes.

Example of Gold Leaf and Palm Leaf Parabaik Manuscripts

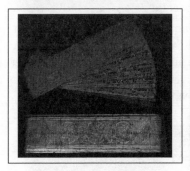

Shwe Pay Chat Gold Leaf Manuscript

Pyu gold Buddhist scriptures are not only important works of art, giving clues to the period's aesthetic learnings, but of acute historical significance. Indeed, being inscribed on gold, the over 1,600 year old texts survived whereas scriptures on paper, bamboo or palm leaf, even of much later manufacture, did not.

MYAZEDI STONE SCRIPT: The earliest Myanmar script carved on stone by Prince Yarza Komer 1112 AD.

Pronouns

After knowing a brief history about Burma and its language, let us talk a bit of Burmese. Most of the people thought that Burmese is not an easy language to learn. But if one follows strictly to the rules, it can become an easy language and an interesting one too. Before we start, let us look at the pronouns first. Here you should bear in mind that in Burmese language, pronouns are used according to gender and also according to the difference in age or status between the addressor and the addressee.

Pronouns	Male	Female
I	*kyanaw* ကျွန်တော်	*kyama* ကျွန်မ
You	*khin bya:* ခင်ဗျား	*shin* ရှင်
Your	*khin bya:* ခင်ဗျား	*shin* ရှင်
We	*kyanawdo* ကျွန်တော်တို့	*Kyamado* ကျွန်မတို့
He/She	*thu* သူ	*thu/thuma* သူမ
His/Her	*thu* သူ့	*thuma* သူမ
They	*thudo* သူတို့	*thudo* သူတို့

Among very close friends or relatives or speaking to juniors one can use intimate terms as:

I	*nga* (for both sexes)	ငါ
You	*nin/min*	မင်း၊ နင် ။
We	*ngado*	ငါတို့ ။
They	*nindo/mindo*	နင်တို့၊ မင်းတို့ ။

39

Time
A-chain
အချိန်။

Now
A gu
အခု

Later
Nao ma
နောက်မှ

Before
A yin
အရင်

Morning
Ma ne
မနက်

Afternoon
Nei le
နေ့လည်

Night
Nya
ည

Clock time
A-chain-na-yi
အချိန်နာရီ။

"What time is it now?"
"Akhu bae achain shi byi lae`?"
"It's 8:30."
"Shit naryi khwe byi."

What time is it?
Be na nai to bi le?
ဘယ်နှစ်နာရီ ထိုးပြီလဲ

It is nine in the morning.
Ko nai to bi.
ကိုးနာရီထိုးပြီ

41

Three-thirty p.m.
Thoun nar yi khwe.
သုံးနာရီခွဲ

Duration

Minute(s)
Min-ni
မိနစ်

Hour(s)
Na yi
နာရီ

Day(s)
Ye' or nei
ရက် ။ နေ့

Week(s)
Ba
ပတ်

Month(s)
La
လ

Year(s)
Hni
နှစ်

Days
Yet-myar:
ရက်များ။

Today
Di nei
ဒီနေ့.

Yesterday
Ma nei
မနေ့.

Tomorrow
Ma ne pyan
မနက်ဖြန်

This week
Di ba
ဒီပတ်

Last week
A yin ba
အရင်ပတ်

Next week
Nao ba
နောက်ပတ်

Sunday
Tha nin ga nei
တနင်္ဂနွေနေ့.

Monday
Tha nin la
တနင်္လာနေ့.

Tuesday
In ga
အင်္ဂါ

Wednesday
Bo ta hu
ဗုဒ္ဓဟူး

Thursday
Kya tha ba dei
ကြာသပတေး

Friday
Tao kya
သောကြာ

Saturday
Sa nei
စနေ

Note: The Burmese calendar consists of 8 days, with one day between Wednesday and Thursday, called *ya-hu*, although this is purely ceremonial.

How many days are there in a week?
Ta-pat hma bei hnit yet shi the le`.
တစ်ပတ်မှာ ဘယ်နှစ်ရက်ရှိသလဲ။

There are seven days in a week.
Ta-pat hma khun hnit yet shi bar de.
တစ်ပတ်မှာ ခုနှစ်ရက်ရှိပါတယ်။

Q: What day is today?
    Di nay bar nay le`.
    ဒီနေ့ ဘာနေ့ လဲ။

A: Today is Monday.
    Di nay Ta-nin lar nay bar.
    ဒီနေ့ တနလၤာနေ့ ပါ။

Q: What day was yesterday?
    Ma-nay ga bar nay le`.
    မနေ့က ဘာနေ့ လဲ။

A: Yesterday was Sunday.
    Ma-nay ga Ta-nin-ga-nwe nay bar.
    မနေ့က တနင်္ဂနွေနေ့ ပါ။

Q: What day will be tomorrow?
    Ma-net-pyan bar nay le`.
    မနက်ဖြန် ဘာနေ့ လဲ။

A: Tomorrow will be Tuesday.
    Ma-net-pyan In-gar nay bar.
    မနက်ဖြန် အင်္ဂါနေ့ ပါ။

Colours

A-yaon Mya:

အရောင်များ။

ချုတို့ နှစ်ယောက်ကို
ကြည့်ပါ။
ချုတို့ နာမည်တွေက
မောင်အေး နဲ့ မောင်တင်ပါ။

မောင်အေး လုံချည် အစိမ်း
ဝတ်တယ်။
မောင်တင် လုံချည် အနီ
ဝတ်တယ်။

မောင်အေးမှာ
ဖတ်စရာစာအုပ်ရှိတယ်။
မောင်တင်မှာ
ဖတ်စရာစာအုပ် မရှိပါဘူး။

"Look at those two."
"Thudoe hnit yauk go kyi bar."
"Their names are Maung Aye and Maung Tin."
"Thudoe namae dwe ga Maung Aye nae Maung Tin bar"
"Maung Aye is wearing green longyi."
"Maung Aye longyi asame wut tae."
Maung Tin is wearing red longyi.
"Maung Tin longyi ani wut tae."
"Maung Aye has a book to read."
"Maung Aye mhar phatsayar sarout shi dae."
"Maung Tin does not have a book to read."
"Maung Tin mhar phatsayar sarout ma shi bar bu."

Black
A me yaon
အမဲရောင်

White
A pyu yaon
အဖြူရောင်

Gray
Mi go yaon
မီးခိုးရောင်

Red
A ni yaon
အနီရောင်

Blue
A pya yaon
အပြာရောင်

Yellow
A wa yaon
အဝါရောင်

Green
A sein yaon
အစိမ်းရောင်

Orange
Lein mau yaon
လိမ္မော်ရောင်

Purple
Ka-yan yaon
ခရမ်းရောင်

Brown
A nyo yaon
အညိုရောင်

Do you have it in another colour?
Di hmar nao htat a yaon she they: lar?
ဒီမှာ နောက်ထပ် အရောင် ရှိသေးလား

Money

Ngwe-kyay

ငွေကြေး။

How much is it?
Zey beh lout le?
ဈေး ဘယ်လောက်လဲ

One Myanmar kyat
Deh kyat
တစ်ကျပ်

Two Myanmar kyats
Neh kyat
နှစ်ကျပ်

Three Myanmar kyats
Thone kyat
သုံးကျပ်

Four Myanmar kyats
Ley kyat
လေးကျပ်

Five Myanmar kyats
Nga kyat
ငါးကျပ်

Six Myanmar kyats
Chowt kyat
ခြောက်ကျပ်

Seven Myanmar kyats
Cuni kyat
ခုနစ်ကျပ်

Eight Myanmar kyats
Sheh kyat
ရှစ်ကျပ်

Nine Myanmar kyats
Coh kyat
ကိုးကျပ်

Ten Myanmar kyats
Se kyat
တစ်ဆယ်

Twenty Myanmar kyats
Neh se kyat
နှစ်ဆယ်

Twenty-five Myanmar kyats
Neh se nga kyat
နှစ်ဆယ် ငါးကျပ်

or more commonly

Fifty Myanmar kyats
A sait
အစိတ်
Nga se kyat
ငါးဆယ်ကျပ်

One hundred Myanmar kyats
Tayar kyat
တစ်ရာကျပ်

When referring to US currency, it is important to remember to say "dollar" before the specified amount. For example US$50 would be *"dollar nga se"*.

Weather

Yar-Thi-Oo-Tu

ရာသီဥတု။

Q: How is the weather today?
Di nay yar-thi-oo-tu bei lo le`?
ဒီနေ့ရာသီဥတု ဘယ်လိုလဲ။

A: Today the weather is pleasant/fine.
Di nay yar-thi-oo-tu tar yar_de`./kaung de`.
ဒီနေ့ ရာသီဥတု သာယာတယ်။ ကောင်းတယ်။

hot
pu de`.
ပူတယ်။

cold
ee de`
အေးတယ်။

raining
Moe-ywa de`
မိုးရွာတယ်။

cloudy
Moe-oun de`
မိုးအုံ့တယ်။

Q: Do you think it is going to rain?
Moe-ywa me` htin ta lar?
မိုးရွာမယ် ထင်သလား။

A: Think so.
htin de`.
ထင်တယ်॥

Don't think so.
Ma htin bu.
မထင်ဘူး॥

Look..... It has started raining.
Haw..... Moe ywa lar pyi.
ဟော..... မိုးရွာလာပြီ॥

Look..... It has stopped raining.
Haw..... Moe tei`twa pyi.
ဟော..... မိုးတိတ်သွားပြီ॥

Q: Do you feel cold?
Aye ta lar/Chan ta lar?
အေးသလား၊ ချမ်းသလား॥

A: It is cold.
Aye de`/Chan de`.
အေးတယ်၊ ချမ်းတယ်॥

It is not cold.
Ma aye bu:/Ma chan bu.
မအေးဘူး၊ မချမ်းဘူး॥

Q: Do you like hot weather?
Pu de`yar thi ko kyaik the lar:?
ပူတဲ့ ရာသီကို ကြိုက်သလား॥

A: Like.
Kyaik te`.
ကြိုက်တယ်॥

Don't like.
Ma kyaik bu:.
မကြိုက်ဘူး။

Q: Which weather do you like?
Be` yar thi ko kyaik the le:?
ဘယ်ရာသီကို ကြိုက်သလဲ။

A: I like cold weather.
Ee de` yar thee go kyaik te`.
အေးတဲ့ ရာသီကို ကြိုက်တယ်။

Parts Of The Body
Ko Inga Aseik Apaing Myar
ကိုယ်အဂါ့ အစိတ်အပိုင်းများ။

Face
Myet Hnar
မျက်နှာ

Eye
Myet Se
မျက်စေ့

Eyebrow
Myet Khone Hmwe
မျက်ခုံးမွှေး

Forehead
Nah-phoo
နဖူး

Nose
Nah khong
နှာခေါင်း

Mouth
Pa-zat
ပါးစပ်

Lips
Hnah-khan
နှုတ်ခမ်း

Teeth
Thwah
သွား

Tongue
Sha
လျှာ

Cheek
Pah
ပါး

Chin
May:zee
မေးစေ့

Ear
Nah: (nah-yooet)
နား။ နားရွက်

Hair
Za-bin
ဆံပင်

Neck
Lei-bin:
လည်ပင်း

Throat
Lei-jowng
လည်ချောင်း

Shoulder
Pa-khone
ပခုံး

Arm
Let-maung:
လက်မောင်း

Hand
Let
လက်

Fingers
Let-chaung:
လက်ချောင်း

Chest
Yin-bhat
ရင်ဘတ်

Stomach
Wan-baik
ဝမ်းဗိုက်

Navel
Chet
ချက်

Waist
Khaa
ခါး

Buttocks
Tin-bar
တင်ပါး

Thighs
Paung
ပေါင်

Knee
Doo
ဒူး

Leg
Chay-douk
ခြေထောက်

Toes
Chay-chaung
ခြေချောင်း

Transportation:
Bus, Train, Ship and Plane
Thae-u-po-saung-yay:
သယ်ယူပို့ဆောင်ရေး။

"What is the name of this street?"
"Di lann namae bae lo khaw tha lae`?"
"It is called Lanmadaw."
"Lann ma daw loe khaw bar dae."

Train
Yeh-ta
ရထား။

Train Station
Bhu ta yone
ဘူတာရုံ

Bus
Ba(sa) ka
ဘတ်စ်ကား

Bus Stop
Ka hma tine
ကား မှတ်တိုင်

Bus Station
Ka gait
ကားဂိတ်

Ship
Thin bau
သင်္ဘော

Port
Thin bau sey
သင်္ဘောဆိပ်

Aeroplane
Leyin pyan
လေယာဉ်ပျံ

Airport
Ley seik
လေဆိပ်

Ticket
Leh hma
လက်မှတ်

Fare
Ka kha
ကား ခ

Depart/Leave
Tweh
သွား

Arrive
Yow
ရောက်

Luggage
Pyit see
ပစ္စည်း

Eating
Sar-thauk-chin:
စားသောက်ခြင်း။

Eat
Sar bar
စားပါ

Please eat.
Sar bar ohn.
စားပါဦး

Will you eat?
Sar ma lar?
စားမလား။

Is it good to eat?
Sar loe kaung lar?
စားလို့ကောင်းလား။

I am hungry.
Nga bite sa de.
ငါဗိုက်ဆာတယ်။

Where do you want to eat?
Beh sau thot sine thwa meh le?
ဘယ်စားသောက်ဆိုင်သွားမလဲ

I can only drink bottled water.
Kha naw ye bu ye be thouk lo ya de.
ကျွန်တော် ရေဘူးရေတဲ့ သောက်လို့ရတယ်

Are there any napkins? (Can I have one?)
Lathoat puwar she tha la?
လက်သုတ်ပုဝါ ရှိသလား။

The Myanmar family usually eat their meals on a round table. The first choice morsel goes to father, but it somehow gets back to the tiniest tot or others in turn. The parents eat sparingly if they are not affluent. But if you listen to the chatter and banter at the dinner table, the father will tease one or the other of the children. Myanmar children can be mischievous and deliberately let cats out of the bag.

Rice and Curry
Hta min nae hin
ထမင်း နှင့် ဟင်း။

Rice
Hta min
ထမင်း

Coconut rice
Ohn hta min
အုန်းထမင်း

Glutinous rice cooked in oil
Si hta min
ဆီထမင်း

Butter rice
Htaw but hta min
ထောပတ်ထမင်း

Salad rice
Hta min thoat
ထမင်းသုတ်

Pilau Rice
Dan bout hta min
ဒန်ပေါက်ထမင်း

Fried foods
Uh chaw sa
အကြော်စာ

Noodles
Cow sweh
ခေါက်ဆွဲ

Fried rice
Hta min chaw
ထမင်းကြော်

Cooked rice
Hta min phyu
ထမင်းဖြူ

Glutinous rice
Cout hnyin
ကောက်ညှင်း

Curry
Hin
ဟင်း

Soup
Hin cho
ဟင်းချို

Vegetable
Hin thee hin ywet
ဟင်းသီးဟင်းရွက်

Thai soup
Yoe da yar hin cho
ယိုးဒယားဟင်းချို

Fish head soup
Nyar goung hin cho
ငါးခေါင်းဟင်းချို

(12) Variety soup
Set hna myo hin cho
(၁၂) မျိုး ဟင်းချို

Pork curry
Wet thar hin
ဝက်သားဟင်း

Beef curry
Ah mare thar hin
အမဲသားဟင်း

Chicken curry
Kyet thar hin
ကြက်သားဟင်း

Mutton curry
Sate thar hin
ဆိတ်သားဟင်း

Fish curry
Ngar hin
ငါးဟင်း

Fried greens
Hin ywet kyaw
ဟင်းရွက်ကြော်

Pork liver curry
Wet ca li zar hin
ဝက်ကလီဇာဟင်း

Mutton liver curry
Sate ca li zar hin
ဆိတ်ကလီဇာဟင်း

Ice
Yey ghe
ရေခဲ

Ice cream bar
Yey ghe mou
ရေခဲမုန့်.

Sugar
De ja
သကြား

Salt
Sa
ဆား

MSG
A cho mout
အချိုမှုန့်.

Potato
Ah lou
အာလူး

Vegetable
A yweh
အရွက်

Fruit
A thee
အသီး

Banana
Nguh pyaw thee
ငှက်ပျောသီး

Apple
Pun thee
ပန်းသီး

Apple juice
Pun thee yay
ပန်းသီးရည်

Grapes
Zapyit thee
စပျစ်သီး

Durian
Doo hinh thee
ဒူးရင်းသီး

Orange
Lei maw thee
လိမ္မော်သီး

Chicken
Chet tha
ကြက်သား

Beef
Ameh tha
အမဲသား

68

Goat
Seit tha
ဆိတ်သား

Lamb
Tho tha
သိုးသား

Fish
Nga
ငါး

At A Restaurant
Hta-min Saing Mhar.
ထမင်းဆိုင်မှာ။

"What is this?"
"Da bar lae?"
"This is a restaurant."
"Da htamin saine bar"
"What kind of restaurant is this?
"Bae loe htamin saine lae?"
"This is a Myanmar restaurant."
"Myanmar sarthauk saine bar"
"What will you eat?
"Bar sar ma lae?"
I will eat noodles."
"Khauk swe sar mae"
"What meat will you eat with?"
"Bar athar nae lae?"
"I will try chicken."
"Kyatha nae sar mae"

Waiter
Za-pwe htoe
စားပွဲထိုး

70

In this conversation the Waiter will be referred as W and the Customer will be referred as C.

"Please eat slowly. Don't worry."
"Phaye phaye sar bar. Ar ma nar bar nae."
"Yes, I am not used to eating fast."
"Hokae kyunaw amyan ma sar tat bar bu."
Try lots of chicken curry.
"Kyatha mya: mya: sar bar."
"Ok."
"Hokae."

W: With what curry you want to eat?
   Bar hin ne. sar: ma le`?
   ဘာဟင်းနဲ့ စားမလဲ။

C: What curries do you have?
   Bar hin dwe shi tha le`?
   ဘာဟင်းတွေရှိသလဲ။

W: There are variety of curries: chicken curry, fish curry, mutton curry, prawn curry, fried vegetables, fried egg, steam fish, soup.

Hin dwe soun bar de. Kyet thar hin, nga: hin, seik thar hin,
pazun hin, hin thee hin ywet kyaw, kyet-u-kyaw, Nga: paun,
hin cho shi de`.

ဟင်းတွေစုံပါတယ်။ ကြက်သားဟင်း၊ ငါးဟင်း၊ ဆိတ်သားဟင်း၊
ပုစွန်ဟင်း၊ ဟင်းသီးဟင်းရွက်ကြော်၊ ကြက်ဥကြော်၊ ငါးပေါင်း၊
ဟင်းချို ရှိပါတယ်။

C: Can I get fried rice?
Hta min kyaw ya ma lar?
ထမင်းကြော်ရမလား။

W: You can order it.
Hma yin ya ba de`.
မှာရင်ရပါတယ်။

C: Ok, give me a plate of fried rice.
Kaung bi, hta min kyaw tit pwe pay ba.
ကောင်းပြီ၊ ထမင်းကြော်တစ်ပွဲပေးပါ။

W: What would you like to drink?
Bar tauk ma le`?
ဘာသောက်မလဲ။

C: I would like to drink water, coke, orange juice, tea, coffee, milk.
Ye, coke, leinmaw ye`, letphat ye, kapi, nwa no. tauk me`.
ရေ၊ ကုတ်၊ လိမ္မော်ရေ၊ လက်ဖက်ရေ၊ ကော်ဖီ၊ နွားနို့၊ သောက်မယ်။

W: What do you like to order more?
Naut bar hma oun ma le`.
နောက် ဘာမှာအုံးမလဲ။

C: Nothing else, just give me tissue.
Ma hma dau. bar bu: Tisu be` pay bar.
မမှာတော့ပါဘူး၊ တီရှူးဘဲပေးပါ။

72

W: Yes
Houk ke`.
ဟုတ်ကဲ့။

Dinner At The Hotel
Hote` Twin Nya Zar Sar Chin
ဟိုတယ်တွင် ညစာစားခြင်း။

I have a small party for dinner tonight.
Di nae nya kyundaw nya zar sar pwe tiq khu go thaw phyo. shi bar dae.
ဒီနေ.ည ကျွန်တော် ညစာစားပွဲတစ်ခုကို သွားဖို့ရှိပါတယ်။

We wish to eat Chinese food.
Kyundaw toe har tayoke asar:asar sar chin seik shi bar dae.
ကျွန်တော်တို့ဟာ တရုတ်အစားအစာ စားချင်စိတ်ရှိပါတယ်။

We also want to eat some Burmese food.
Kyundaw toe dwe Myanmar asar:asar tiq cho go lae sar chin seik shi bar dae.
ကျွန်တော်တို့တွေ မြန်မာအစားအစာတစ်ချို့ကို လည်း စားချင်စိတ်ရှိပါတယ်။

Show me your Menu, please.
Sar thuk phwe yar saryin pya pay bar khinbya.
စားသောက်ဖွယ်ရာ စာရင်းပြပေးပါခင်များ။

I don't know what to choose. What will you suggest?
Kyundaw bar go yawe ya mhan ma thi bu. Khin bya akyan pyu bar oo?
ကျွန်တော် ဘာကို ရွေးရမှန်းမသိဘူး။ ခင်များ အကြံပြုပါဦး။

Can we dine in this room?
Kyundaw doe di akhan mhar nyazar sar loe ya tha lar?
ကျွန်တော်တို့ ဒီအခန်းမှာ ညစာစားလို့ရသလား။

I want to eat something right now.
Kyundaw akhu lawlaw sae tiq khu khu sar loe. ya ma lar.
ကျွန်တော် အခုလောလောဆယ် တစ်ခုခု စားလို့ရမလား။

I am very hungry.
Kyundaw ayan sar nay byi.
ကျွန်တော် အရမ်းဆာနေပြီ။

I want a plate of ....
Tiq pangan lauk ya ma lar ....
.... တစ်ပန်းကန်လောက်ရမလား။

Mohingar
Mohinkha
မုန့်ဟင်းခါး

Fried rice with chicken
Kyetha htamin gyaw
ကြက်သားထမင်းကြော်

Fried sweet and sour fish
Nga kyaw cho chin
ငါးကြော်ချိုချဉ်

Fried fish in gravy
Nga kyaw nae hin ahnit
ငါးကြော်နဲ့ဟင်းအနှစ်

75

Steamed fish
Nga paung
ငါးပေါင်း

Boiled prawns and chilli sauce
Pazun byuk nae ngayoke chin
ပုဇွန်ပြုတ်နဲ့ ငရုပ်ချဉ်

At A Bar

Aphaw-ya-ma-kar Kaung-tar
အဖျော်ယမကာ ကောင်တာ။

Beer/Alcohol
Ayet
အရက်

Round (as in "A round of beers")
Wine pweh
ဝိုင်းဖွဲ့.

Cigarettes
Sei lait
ဆေးလိပ်

Glass
Phan kwut
ဖန်ခွက်

Terms Of Address
A-khaw-a-wor A-thone-a-hnone
အခေါ်အဝေါ် အသုံးအနှုန်း။

"Are you Daw Ma Ma?"
"Khinbya, Daw Ma Ma lar?"
"Yes, I am Daw Ma Ma."
"Hoke kae kyunma Daw Ma Ma bar."
"Are they U Ba Khin and Daw Thuza there?"
"Ho mhar, U Ba Khin nae Daw Thuzar lar?"

To a man considerably older than yourself
U sounds as *Oo* (Mr.)
ဦး

To a woman older than yourself
Daw (Madam)
ဒေါ်

78

To a man your own age or older
Ko (Brother)
ကို

To a woman your own age or younger
Ma (Miss)
မ

To a man your own age or younger
Maung (Younger Brother)
မောင်

Introducing
Meik-set-chin:
မိတ်ဆက်ခြင်း။

မိတ်ဆက်ပေးမယ်နော်

ကျွန်တော်တို့ နာမည်က
မောင်ထွန်းတင့်နဲ့ မသောင်းစီပါ။

သူတို့ နာမည်က
ကိုခင်မောင်ညိုနဲ့ မရင်ရင်ပါ။

ကျွန်တော်တို့
မိတ်ဆွေ တွေပါ။

"Let me introduce."
"Mate set pay mae naw."
"We are Maung Tun Tint and Ma Thaung Si."
"Kyun naw doe namae ga Maung Tun Tint nae`.
Ma Thaung Si bar."
"They are Ko Khin Maung Nyo and Ma Yin Yin."
"Thudoe namae ga Ko Khin Maung Nyo nae`. Ma Yin Yin bar."
"We are friends."
"Kyundaw doe mate swe dwe bar."

Good morning.
Mingalarbar.
မင်္ဂလာပါ။

How are you?
Nay kaung lar?
နေကောင်းလား။

Fine, thank you.
Kaung bar dae. Kyaye zu tin bar dae.
ကောင်းပါတယ်။ ကျေးဇူးတင်ပါတယ်။

May I introduce myself. I am Maung Maung. May I know your name please?
Kya naw mate set par ya zay. Kya naw ga Maung Maung bar. Khinbya name go thi bar ya zay?
ကျွန်တော် မိတ်ဆက်ပါရစေ။ ကျွန်တော် က မောင်မောင် ပါ။ ခင်ဗျား နာမည် ကို သိပါရစေ။

My name is John Smith.
Kya naw name ga John Smith par.
ကျွန်တော်နာမည် ဂျွန်စမစ်သ် ပါ။

Nice to see you.
Twaie ya dar won thar bar dae.
တွေ့ရတာ ဝမ်းသာပါတယ်။

Same to you.
Kya naw lae won thar bar dae.
ကျွန်တော်လည်း ဝမ်းသာ ပါတယ်။

From which country are you?
Khinbya ga bae taing pyi ga lae`?
ခင်ဗျား က ဘယ်တိုင်းပြည်က လဲ။

I am from London.
Kya naw London ga bar.
ကျွန်တော် လန်ဒန် ကပါ။

81

Have you been to Myanmar before?
Ayin ga Myanmar pyay go yauk phoo tha lar?
အရင်က မြန်မာပြည်ကို ရောက်ဖူးသလား။

No, this is the first time for me.
Ma yauk phoo bar boo. Dar har kya naw atwet pa tha ma zone akyane bar bae`.
မရောက်ဖူးပါဘူး။ ဒါဟာ ကျွန်တော်အတွက် ပထမဆုံး အကြိမ်ပါဘဲ။

How do you find the weather?
Yarthi oo du ga yaw bae lo nay lae`?
ရာသီဥတုကရော ဘယ်လိုနေလဲ။

The weather is fine.
Yarthi oo du ga kaung bar dae.
ရာသီဥတု က ကောင်းပါတယ်။

Which place is hotter, Yangon or Mandalay?
Yangon nae Mandalay bae har po pu tha lae`?
ရန်ကုန် နဲ့ မန္တလေး ဘယ်ဟာ ပိုပူသလဲ။

Mandalay is hotter than Yangon.
Mandalay ga Yangon htet po pu bar dae.
မန္တလေး က ရန်ကုန်ထက် ပိုပူပါတယ်။

Greetings And Saying Goodbye
Hno` Set
နှုတ်ဆက်။

1. Azlan : Good morning, teacher.
   Mingalabar Sayarma.
   မင်္ဂလာပါဆရာမ။

   Sayarma : Good morning, Azlan.
   Mingalabar Azlan.
   မင်္ဂလာပါ အဇ်လန်။

2. Sayarma : How are you?
   Nay kaun: lar:?
   နေကောင်းလား။

   Azlan : I am fine. Thank you.
   Kaun: bar de`. Kyei: zu: tin bar de`.
   ကောင်းပါတယ်။ ကျေးဇူးတင်ပါတယ်။

3. Azlan : Teacher, how are you?
   Sayarma gaw nay kaun: lar:
   ဆရာမကော နေကောင်းလား။

   Sayarma : I am fine. Thank you.
   Kaun: bar de`. Kyei: zu: tin bar de`.
   ကောင်းပါတယ်။ ကျေးဇူးတင်ပါတယ်။

4. Sayarma : Have you eaten, Azlan?
   Sar: pi bi lar:, Azlan?
   စားပြီးပြီလား အဇ်လန်။

Azlan	:	I have eaten. I am going now, excuse me teacher.

Sar: pi bi. Thwa bar oun me`, kwint pyu bar sayarma.

စားပြီးပြီ။ သွားပါအုံးမယ်။ ခွင့်ပြုပါ ဆရာမ။

5. Sayarma	:	Alright. Take care.

Kaun: bi. Kaun: kaun: thwa naw.

ကောင်းပြီ။ ကောင်းကောင်းသွားနော်။

Azlan	:	Yes, I will.

Houk ke`.

ဟုတ်ကဲ့။

6. Sayarma	:	See you again.

Nauk twe da paw`.

နောက်တွေ့တာပေါ့။

Azlan	:	Yes, I am leaving teacher.

Houk ke`. Thwa bi sayama.

ဟုတ်ကဲ့။ သွားပြီဆရာမ။

Interrogatives
Ah May:
အမေး

In Burmese language, any type of questions will end up with the word "*lar:* or *le*'". So if you happen to see any of these two words at the end of a sentence, you should know that it is a question. Regarding these two words, one thing the students always ask is: 'How am I suppose to know when to use one of these two words?'. It is simple. If you want a definite answer using 'yes' or 'no', you should ask with *'lar:'* in your question and if you want an answer with description, use *le*'.

Examples:

1. Q: Have you eaten?
        Sar: pi bi lar?
        စားပြီးပြီလား။

    A: Yes.
        Houk ke'
        ဟုတ်ကဲ့။

2. Q: Do you understand?
        Na: le la:?
        နားလည်လား။

    A: Yes/No.
        Houk ke/Hin. In:
        ဟုတ်ကဲ့။/ဟင့်အင်း။

3. Q: Are (you) a student?
         Kyaun: dha:/Kyaun: dhu la:?
         ကျောင်းသား။ ကျောင်းသူလား။

    A: Yes/No.
         Houk ke/Hin. in:
         ဟုတ်ကဲ့။/ဟင့်အင်း။

4. Q: Do (you) like it?
         Da kyaik la:?
         ဒါကြိုက်လား။

    A: Yes/No.
         Houk ke/Hin. in:
         ဟုတ်ကဲ့။/ဟင့်အင်း။

5. Q: With what did you eat?
         Bar ne' sar: the le`?
         ဘာနဲ့စားသလဲ။

    A: With fish.
         Nga: ne' sar de`.
         ငါးနဲ့စားတယ်။

What
Ba le
ဘာလဲ။

Where
Bei hma
ဘယ်မှာ

Where to
Bei go
ဘယ်ကို

Who
Bei thu
ဘယ်သူ

When
Bei daw
ဘယ်တော့

How
Bei lo
ဘယ်လို

How much
Bei lauk
ဘယ်လောက်

Why
Bar phyit lo/Bar gyaunt
ဘာဖြစ်လို့၊ ဘာကြောင့်။

Which
Bei ha
ဘယ်ဟာ

1. **What**
   Ba le:
   ဘာလဲ။

   What's that?
   Da ba le:?
   ဒါဘာလဲ။

   What did (you) say?
   Ba pyo: da le:?
   ဘာပြောသလဲ။

   What did he say?
   Thu ba pyo: da le:?
   သူဘာပြောသလဲ။

   What do (you) want to eat?
   Ba sa: jin le:?
   ဘာစားချင်လဲ။

   What do (you) want to drink
   Ba thauk jin le:?
   ဘာသောက်ချင်လဲ။

2. **Where**
   Be hma le:
   ဘယ်မှာလဲ။

   Where is the Malaysian Embassy?
   Malaysia than youn: be hma le:?
   မလေးရှား သံရုံးဘယ်မှာလဲ။

Where is the bus stop?
Ka: gait be hma le:?
ကားဂိတ်ဘယ်မှာလဲ။

Where is the hospital?
Hsay: youn be hma le:?
ဆေးရုံ ဘယ်မှာလဲ။

Where is the police station?
Ye: sa-khan be hma le:?
ရဲစခန်း ဘယ်မှာလဲ။

Where is the public toilet?
Pyi dhu ein dha be hma le:?
ပြည်သူ့အိမ်သာ ဘယ်မှာလဲ။

3. **Who**
   Ba thu le:
   ဘယ်သူလဲ။

   Who are you?
   Kha-mya:/shin be thu le:?
   ခင်ဗျား။ ရှင်ဘယ်သူလဲ။

   Who is there?
   Ho ha ba thu le:?
   ဟိုဟာဘယ်သူလဲ။

   Who are (you) looking for?
   Ba thu go sha nay da le:?
   ဘယ်သူ့ကို ရှာနေသလဲ။

Who is he/she?
Thu ba thu le:?
သူဘယ်သူလဲ॥

4. **When**

   Be daw. (future)/Be doun: ga. (past)
   ဘယ်တော့॥ ဘယ်တုန်းက॥

   When will (you) come?
   Be daw. la hma le:?
   ဘယ်တော့လာမှာလဲ॥

   When will (you) go back?
   Be daw. pyan hma le:?
   ဘယ်တော့ ပြန်မှာလဲ॥

   When will (you) have dinner?
   Nya. za be daw. sa: hma le:?
   ညစာဘယ်တော့စားမှာလဲ॥

   When did (you) arrive?
   Be doun: ga yauk tha le:?
   ဘယ်တုန်းကရောက်သလဲ॥

5. **How**

   Ba-lo/Ba-lauk
   ဘာလို့॥ ဘာလောက်॥

   How old are (you)?
   A thet ba lauk shi. bi le:?
   အသက်ဘယ်လောက်ရှိပြီလဲ॥

How long have (you) been here?
Di hma nay da ba lauk kya bi le:?
ဒီမှာ နေတာဘယ်လောက် ကြာပြီလဲ။

How can (I) go there?
Ho go be lo thwa ya hma le:?
ဟိုကိုဘယ်လိုသွားရမှာလဲ။

6. **How much**
   Be lauk le:
   ဘယ်လောက်လဲ။

   How much is it?
   E` da be lauk le:?
   အဲဒါဘယ်လောက်လဲ။

7. **Why**
   Be phyit lo. ....le:
   ဘာဖြစ်လို့..........လဲ။

   Why don't you come?
   Ba phyit lo. ma la tha le:?
   ဘာဖြစ်လို့မလာသလဲ။

   Why (you) forget about it?
   E` da go ba phyit lo. may. tha le:?
   အဲဒါ ကိုဘာဖြစ်လို့မေ့သလဲ။

8. **Which**

Be a ya/myi the a ya
ဘယ်အရာ။ မည်သည့်.အရာ။

Which color of it?
Be a yaun le:?
ဘယ်အရောင်လဲ။

Which one do (you) prefer?
Be ha go po kyaik tha le:?
ဘယ်ဟာကို ပိုကြိုက်သလဲ။

The Use of the Negative

The merely word for not is မ *mah*, and it instantly lead the main verb; thus:

> I do not want to eat.
> *Kyundaw mah sar jin bu:*
> ကျွန်တော် မစားချင်ဘူး

The *bu:* at the end is a strong assertive affix generally used with not, and if the sence of never is required စ *tsa* must be placed before it:

> You havent't been here.
> *Nin ma lar sha phoo:*
> နင်မလာစဖူး။

To make it still stronger we may double the ဖူး and say *nga mah sar sa phoo:bu:* ငါမစားစဖူးဘူး Before is expressed by placing *hmee* မှီ and *khin* ခင် after the verb; thus:

Before (he) arrived
Mah yowk hmee
မရောက်မှီ

Before (he) go
Mah thwa gin
မသွားခင်

Without is expressed by placing တဲ့ be after the verb; thus, မပြောတဲ့ mah pyaw be, without telling (it). Yes and No. There is no direct negative like the English No, but the verb hoke, to be true, is used; thus:

It is true, yes.
Hoke thee. or *Hoke ke*`.
ဟုတ်သည် or ဟုတ်ကဲ့.

It is not true, no.
Mah hoke phoo:
မဟုတ်ဖူး

It is not proper to do.
Pyu aut thee mah hoke.
ပြုအပ်သည် မဟုတ်॥

Model of Verb

Infinitive
To eat.

93

Sar-thee.
စားသည်။

Present Continuous Tense

I eat or I am eating.
Nga sar-thee.
ငါစားသည်။

Nga sar nay-thee.
ငါစားနေသည်။

Simple Past Tense

I ate.
Nga sar hkeh-thee.
ငါစားခဲ့သည်။

Present Perfect Tense

I have eaten.
Nga sar pyi.
ငါစားပြီ။

Past Perfect Tense

I had eaten.
Nga sar phoo: pyi.
ငါစားဖူးပြီ။

Simple Future Tense

I will eat.
Nga sar myi.
ငါစားမည်။

Future Perfect Tense

I shall have eaten.

Nga sar pyi lake myi.

ငါစားပြီးလိမ့်မည်။

Use of Possibility

I can eat.

Nga sar hnaing-thee.

ငါစားနိုင်သည်။

Imperative

Eat.

Sar taw.

စားတော့။

Let (him) eat.

Sar say.

စားစေ။

Let us eat.

Sar kya-zoh.

စားကြစို့။

Please eat (it).

Sar par daw.

စားပါတော့။

Civilities (1)
Yi Mon Thaw Zagar Pyaw Khan (1)
ရည်မွန်သော စကားပြောခန်း (၁)

1. Sayarma : Have you eaten, Azlan?
   Sar: pi bi lar: Azlan?
   စားပြီးပြီလား အဇ်လန်॥

   Azlan : Have eaten, teacher.
   Sar: pi bi, sayarma.
   စားပြီးပြီ ဆရာမ॥

   Haven't eaten yet, teacher.
   Masar:te` bu:, sayarma.
   မစားသေးဘူး ဆရာမ॥

2. Sayarma : With what did you eat?
   Bar ne' sar: the le`.
   ဘာနဲ့စားသလဲ॥

   Azlan : Eat with chicken.
   Kyet thar ne' sar: de`.
   ကြက်သားနဲ့စားတယ်॥

   Eat with fish.
   Nga: ne' sar: de`.
   ငါးနဲ့စားတယ်॥

   Eat with prawns.
   Pazun ne' sar: de`.
   ပုဇွန်နဲ့ စားတယ်॥

   I eat with beef, mutton, egg, vegetables,
   roti canai, kuey pau, nasi lemak, kya-kuey,
   bread.

Ahmae thar, seit thar, kyet oo, hin thi hin
ywet , htat-ta-yar, Pauk-se, ohn-hta-min,
ei-kyar-kway, paun mon ne'sar. de`.

အမဲသား၊ ဆိတ်သား၊ ကြက်ဥ၊
ဟင်းသီးဟင်းရွက်၊ ထပ်တရာ၊ ပေါက်ဆီ၊
အုန်းထမင်း၊ အီကြာကွေး၊ ပေါင်မုန့်
နဲ့စားတယ်။

3. Sayarma   :   Is it delicious?
                       Sar: lo kaun: lar:?
                       စားလို့ကောင်းလား။

    Azlan   :   Yes it is.
                       Kaun: de` sayarma.
                       ကောင်းတယ် ဆရာမ။

4. Sayarma   :   Where did you eat?
                       Bei hma sar: da le`?
                       ဘယ်မှာ စားသလဲ။

    Azlan   :   I ate at the canteen.
                       Kanteen hma sar: de`.
                       ကင်တင်းမှာ စားတယ်။

                       I ate at a restaurant.
                       Htamin saing hma sar: de`.
                       ထမင်းဆိုင် မှာစားတယ်။

                       I ate at home.
                       Ein hma sar: de`.
                       အိမ်မှာစားတယ်။

Civilities (2)
Yi Mon Thaw Zagar Pyaw Khan (2)
ရည်မွန်သော စကားပြောခန်း (၂)

1. Q: Where are you going?
   Bei thaw: ma le`?
   ဘယ်သွားမလဲ။

   A: I am going to bazaar, to school, to University Malaya, to class, to town, to the cinema.
   Zay go, kyaung go, Malaya Tekkado go, ahtan go, myo go, youk-shin yon go thaw: me`.
   ဈေးကို၊ ကျောင်းကို၊ မလားရာတက္ကသိုလ်ကို၊ အတန်းကို၊ မြို့ကို၊ ရုပ်ရှင်ရုံကို သွားမယ်။

2. Q: From where are you returning?
   Bei ga pyan lar the le`?
   ဘယ်က ပြန်လာသလဲ။

   A: I am coming back from bazaar, school, University Malaya, class, cinema.
   Zay ga, kyaun ga, Malaya Tekkado ga, ahtan ga, myo ga, youk-shin ga pyan lar de`.
   ဈေးက၊ ကျောင်းက၊ မလားရာ တက္ကသိုလ်က၊ အတန်းက၊ မြို့က၊ ရုပ်ရှင်ရုံက ပြန်လာတယ်။

3. Q: What did you buy?
   Bar wei ge' ta le`?
   ဘာဝယ်ခဲ့သလဲ။

A: I bought food, dress, hat, scarf, shoes and books.
Ah sar: ah sar, ein gyi, oo thot, pa war, pha nat, sar oat wei ge' de`.
အစားအစာ၊ အကျီ၊ ဦးထုပ်၊ ပဝါ၊ ဘိနပ်၊ စာအုပ် ဝယ်ခဲ့တယ်။

4.   Q: How much did you pay?
Bei lauk pay ya the le`?
ဘယ်လောက်ပေးရသလဲ။

A: I pay twenty-five kyats eighty pyas.
Hnit se` ngar kyat pya shise`pay ya de`.
နှစ်ဆယ့် ငါးကျပ်ပြားရှစ်ဆယ်ပေးရတယ်။

5.   Q: Quite cheap.
Paw thar be`.
ပေါသားဘဲ။

A: Yes, it is.
Houk ke`.
ဟုတ်ကဲ့။

Civilities (3)
Yi Mon Thaw Zagar Pyaw Khan (3)
ရည်မွန်သော စကားပြောခန်း (၃)

May you be blessed.
Mingalar bar khin mya:
မင်္ဂလာပါ ခင်များ॥

Same to you.
Mingalar bar
မင်္ဂလာပါ॥

Do you know how to speak Burmese?
Khin bya Bama zagar pyaw: tat the lar:?
ခင်များ ဗမာစကားပြောတတ်သလား॥

I know how to speak a bit.
Nei nei par bar pyaw: tat par de`.
နည်းနည်းပါးပါး ပြောတတ်ပါတယ်॥

Where did you learn Burmese?
Bama zagar go bei hma tin yu ta le`?
ဗမာစကားကို ဘယ်မှာ သင်ယူသလဲ॥

I learn at the University of Malaya.
Malaya-Tek-Ka-Do hma tin yu bar de`.
မလားရားတက္ကသိုလ်မှာ သင်ယူပါတယ်॥

Can you read and write?
Phat tat, ye` tat ta lar:.
ဖတ်တတ်၊ ရေးတတ်သလား॥

Do you like to speak Burmese?
Bama Zagar pyaw: ya da kyaik ta lar:.
ဗမာစကားပြောရတာ ကြိုက်သလား॥

I can read and write.
Phat tat, ye` tat par de`.
ဖတ်တတ်၊ ရေးတတ်ပါတယ်॥

I like to speak.
Kyaik par de`.
ကြိုက်ပါတယ်॥

Have you ever been to Myanmar?
Khin bya Myanmar Naing Ngan go yauk phoo da lar:.
ခင်ဗျား မြန်မာနိုင်ငံကို ရောက်ဖူးသလား॥

I have never been to Myanmar. But I would like to visit there.
Ma yauk phu: bar bu. Dar pe me` kyun naw thwa le`chin bar de`.
မရောက်ဖူးပါဘူး၊ ဒါပေမယ့် ကျွန်တော်သွားလည်ချင်ပါတယ်॥

Please come. I will show you around.
Lar ge` bar khin bar. Kyun naw laik pya bar me`.
လာခဲ့ပါခင်ဗျား၊ ကျွန်တော်လိုက်ပြပါမယ်॥

If so, I will surely come.
Di lo so yin kyun naw set set lar ge`bar me`.
ဒီလိုဆိုရင် ကျွန်တော်ဆက်ဆက်လာခဲ့ပါမယ်॥

When are you coming?
Bei tauh lauk lar hma le`.
ဘယ်တော့လောက် လာမှာ လဲ။

Cannot tell yet. I will let you know the date before I come.
Ma pyaw tat tey bu:. Lar me` yet ko kyo pyaw me`.
မပြောတတ်သေးဘူး။ လာမဲ့ရက်ကို ကြိုပြောပါမယ်။

Okay. I will be waiting to receive you.
Kaun bi. Kyun naw lar kyo nay me`.
ကောင်းပြီ၊ ကျွန်တော် လာကြိုနေမယ်။

Thank you, sir.
Kyei: zu: tin bar de` khin mya.
ကျေးဇူးတင်ပါတယ် ခင်ဗျား။

Asking About Oneself

Tayauk Ah Kyaung Tayauk Mae: Myan Chin:

တစ်ယောက်အကြောင်း တစ်ယောက် မေးမြန်းခြင်း။

1. Q: What is your name?
   Shin`/Khin bya: nanme bar le`?
   ရှင့်၊ ခင်ဗျားနာမယ် ဘာလဲ။

   A: My name is Azlan.
   Kyanaw' nanme Azlan bar.
   ကျွန်တော် နာမည် အဇ်လန်ပါ။

2. Q: What is your race?
   Bar lumyo le`?
   ဘာလူမျိုးလဲ။

   A: I am a Malay/Chinese/Tamil.
   Kyanaw Malay/Ta yok/Tamil lumyo bar.
   ကျွန်တော် မလေး၊ တရုတ်၊ တမယ်လ် လူမျိုးပါ။

3. Q: Where do you come from?
   Bei ga lar the le`?
   ဘယ်ကလာသလဲ။

   A: I come from Malaysia.
   Kyanaw Malaysia ga lar bar de`.
   ကျွန်တော် မလေးရှားက လာပါတယ်။

4. Q: Where do you live?
   Bei hma nay the le`?
   ဘယ်မှာ နေသလဲ။

A: I live in Kuala Lumpur.

Kyanaw Kuala Lumpur Myo hma nay de`.

ကျွန်တော် ကွာလာလမ်ပူမြို့မှာ နေတယ်။

5. Q: How old are you?

   Ah thet bei laut shi pi le`?

   အသက်ဘယ်လောက်ရှိပြီလဲ။

   A: I am twenty-one years old.

   Kyanaw` ah thet hnit seh tit hnit shi pi.

   ကျွန်တော်အသက် နှစ်ဆယ့်တစ်နှစ် ရှိပြီ။

6. Q: What is your occupation?

   Bar ah lok lok the le`?

   ဘာအလုပ်လုပ်သလဲ။

   A: I am a student (male)/I am a student (female)

   Kyanaw kyaung (thar bar.)/Kyama kyaung (thu bar.)

   ကျွန်တော် ကျောင်းသားပါ။   ကျွန်မကျောင်းသူပါ။

7. Q: Where do you study?

   Bei hma sar tin the le`?

   ဘယ်မှာ စာသင်သလဲ။

   A: I study in the University of Malaya.

   Malaya tek-ka-do hma sar tin de`.

   မလားရားတက္ကသိုလ်မှာ စာသင်တယ်။

8. Q: What is your ambition?

   Bar phit pho ye yew the le`?

   ဘာဖြစ်ဖို့ ရည်ရွယ်သလဲ။

A: I aim to become a teacher/lecturer/businessman/
ambassador/doctor.

Sayar tit yauk phit pho ye yew de`/ka-thi-ka/kon the/tan
hmu/sayar wun.

ဆရာတစ်ယောက် ဖြစ်ဖို့.ရည်ရွယ်တယ်။ ကထိက၊ ကုန်သည်၊
တပ်မှူး၊ ဆရာဝန်။

Shopping
Zay-wei-htwet-chin
ဈေးဝယ်ထွက်ခြင်း။

Store
Sine
ဆိုင်

Clothes
Ain gee
အကျီ

Pants
Boun bee
ဘောင်းဘီ

Shoes
Punuht
ဖိနပ်

Bra
Bou le
ဘော်လီ

Ring
Lat sout
လက်စွပ်

Socks
Chey sout
ခြေစွပ်

Purse/Wallet
Puh sun eight
ပိုက်ဆံအိတ်

I would like to go shopping.
Kyanaw zay wei thwa chin de`.
ကျွန်တော်ဈေးဝယ်သွားချင်တယ်။

Will you come with me?
Khamya, kyunaw ne` a tu laik ge` bar lar:?
ခင်ဗျား၊ ကျွန်တော်နဲ့ အတူလိုက်ခဲ့ပါလား။

Where is the book store?
Sar oat saing bei hma le`?
စာအုပ်ဆိုင် ဘယ်မှာလဲ။

Where is the pharmacy?
Sei` saing bei hma le`?
ဆေးဆိုင်ဘယ်မှာ လဲ။

Where is the grocery store?
Koun gyauk saing bei hma le`?
ကုန်ခြောက်ဆိုင် ဘယ်မှာလဲ။

Where is the sundry goods shop?
Koun zon saing bei hma le`?
ကုန်စုံဆိုင် ဘယ်မှာလဲ။

Where is the stationery store?
Sar-ye`-kriyar saing bei hma le`?
စာရေးကရိယာဆိုင် ဘယ်မှာလဲ။

Where is the department store?
Koun taik bei hma le`?
ကုန်တိုက်ဘယ်မှာလဲ။

Where is the jewels shop?
Yadanar saing bei hma le`?
ရတနာဆိုင် ဘယ်မှာလဲ။

Where is the goldsmith shop?
Shwe pa dein saing bei hma le`?
ရွှေပန်းတိမ်ဆိုင် ဘယ်မှာလဲ။

Where is the Burmese restaurant?
Bama sar: tauk saing bei hma le`?
ဗမာ စားသောက်ဆိုင် ဘယ်မှာလဲ၊

Do you have ....?
.... *Shi da lar:?*
.... ရှိသလား ။

Do you have a guide book?
Lan hnyun sar oat shi da lar:?
လမ်းညွှန် စာအုပ်ရှိသလား။

Do you have the map of Myanmar?
Myanmar pyi myei boun shi da lar:?
မြန်မာပြည် မြေပုံရှိသလား။

World map
Kaba myei boun
ကမ္ဘာ မြေပုံ ရှိသလား။

Matches
Mi-chit
မီးခြစ်

Cigarettes
Say leik
ဆေးလိပ်

Envelop
Sar eigh
စာအိတ်

Writing pad
Sar-ye-set-ku-kat
စာရေးစက္ကူကတ်

Soap
Sap-pya
ဆပ်ပြာ

Can I see that, please?
Ei da lay kyi.ba ya ze`?
အဲဒါလေး ကြည့်ပါရစေ။

Do you have other colours?
Ta cha: ayaun shi de` lar:?
တခြားအရောင် ရှိသေးလား။

Do you have something better?
Di htet po kaun: da shi de` lar:?
ဒီထက်ပိုကောင်းတာ ရှိသေးလား။

How much is it?
Da bei lauk le:?
ဒါ ဘယ်လောက်လဲ။

That's expensive.
Zay: kyi: lun de.
ဈေးကြီးလွန်းတယ်။

Tell me the lowest price?
A ne`zoun: zay pyaw ba?
အနည်းဆုံးဈေး ပြောပါ။

Ok, I will buy it.
Kaun bi, Kyunaw wei me`.
ကောင်းပြီ၊ ကျွန်တော်ဝယ်မယ်။

Do you accept credit cards?
A Kywe: wei kad ko let khan the lar:?
အကြွေးဝယ်ကဒ်ကို လက်ခံသလား။

A Visitor

Eithe Tiq Yauk

ဧည့်သည် တစ်ယောက်။

Good evening, Mrs. Noto, is your husband at home?

Kaung thaw nya nae gyin bar Mrs. Noto. khinbya yaukya ein mhar shi tha lar:?

ကောင်းသော ညနေခင်းပါ မစ္စစ်နိုတို။ ခင်ဗျားယောက်ျား အိမ်မှာ ရှိသလား။

Yes, Mr. Harun. He got home half an hour ago.

Hokae Mr. Harun. Thu lun gae dae naryi wet ka ein go pyan yauk par dae.

ဟုတ်ကဲ့ မစ္စတာ ဟာရွန်။ သူ လွန်ခဲ့တဲ့နာရီဝက်က အိမ်ကို ပြန်ရောက်ပါတယ်။

I want to borrow a dictionary from him. Do you think he will lend it to me?

Kyundaw thu si ga abidan tiq ouk hnar gyin loe bar. Thu hnar lake mae loe. Khinbya htin bar tha lar?

ကျွန်တော် သူ့ဆီက အဘိဓာန်တစ်အုပ် ငှားချင်လို့ပါ။ သူငှားလိမ့်မယ်လို့ ခင်ဗျားထင်ပါသလား။

Sure, he will. If he has got one. Please come in, Mr. Harun.

Thae char bar dae daw shin. thu mhar ae dar shi yin hnar bar lake mae. kyaezu pyu pyi ahtae go win bar Mr. Harun.

သေချာပါတယ်ရှင်။ သူ့မှာ အဲဒါ ရှိရင် ငှားပါလိမ့်မယ်။ ကျေးဇူးပြုပြီးအထဲကို ဝင်ပါ မစ္စတာ ဟာရွန်။

111

Thank you, Mrs. Noto.
Kyaezu tin bar dae Mrs. Noto.
ကျေးဇူးတင်ပါတယ် မစ္စစ်နိုတို။

Won't you have a seat?
Htaine bar lar shin?
ထိုင်ပါလားရှင်။

Thanks.
Kyaezu tin bar dae.
ကျေးဇူးတင်ပါတယ်

Excuse me for a moment, Mr. Harun. I will tell my husband that you are here.
Khana lauk khwint pu bar Mr. Harun. Kyunma yaukya go shin di mhar yauk nae gyaung pyaw bar ya say.
ခဏလောက်ခွင့်ပြုပါ မစ္စတာ ဟာရွန်။ ကျွန်မ ယောက်ျားကို ရှင် ဒီမှာ ရောက်နေကြောင်း ပြောပါရစေ။

Certainly, Mrs. Noto.
Hoke tar pau, Mrs. Noto.
ဟုတ်တာပေါ့ မစ္စစ်နိုတို။

a few minutes later

Hello, Mr. Noto.
Helo, Mr. Noto.
ဟဲလို မစ္စတာ နိုတို။

I am glad to see you.
Twe ya dar own thar bar dae khinbya.
တွေ့ရတာဝမ်းသာပါတယ် ခင်ဗျား။

I am glad to see you, too, Mr. Harun. What brings you here?
*Kyundaw lae twe ya dar own thar bar dae khinbya. bar kate sa
mya shi bar tha lae khinbya.*

ကျွန်တော်လည်းတွေ့ရတာဝမ်းသါပါတယ်ခင်ဗျား။ ဘာကိစ္စများ
ရှိပါသလဲခင်ဗျား။

I came here to ask you whether you can lend me an English
dictionary.
*Kyundaw lar gae dae akyaun ga khinbya si ga ingalake abidan tiq
ouk hnar gyin loe bar.*

ကျွန်တော်လာခဲ့တဲ့အကြောင်းက ခင်ဗျားဆီက အင်္ဂလိပ်
အဘိဓာန်တစ်အုပ် ငှားချင်လို့ပါ။

Of course. I will lend it to you. Let us go into my study room. I
will find what you want.
*Thay char bar dae. kyudaw khinbya go hnar bar mae. kyundaw
doe sar kyi khan go thwa gya bar soe. Kyundaw khinbya loe gyin
dar go shar pay bar mae.*

သေချာပါတယ်။ ကျွန်တော် ခင်ဗျားကို ငှားပါမယ်။ ကျွန်တော်တို့
စာကြည့်ခန်းကို သွားကြပါစို့။ ကျွန်တော် ခင်ဗျားလိုချင်တာကို
ရှာပေးပါမယ်။

I am so sorry, Mr. Noto. I do not like putting you to so much trouble.
*Won nae bar dae Mr. Noto. Kyundaw khinbya go dokha mya ma
pay gyin bar bu.*

ဝမ်းနည်းပါတယ် မစ္စတာ နိုတို။ ကျွန်တော် ခင်ဗျားကို
ဒုက္ခများမပေးချင်ပါဘူး။

Never mind, Mr. Harun. It is a great pleasure for me. Come this way, please.
Katesa ma shi bar bu Mr. Harun. Da kyundaw. piti tiq khu bar. Kyaezu pyu pyi di lann ga lar gae bar.
ကိစ္စမရှိပါဘူး မစ္စတာ ဟာရွန်။ ဒါ ကျွန်တော်ပိတိ တစ်ခုပါ။ ကျေးဇူးပြုပြီး ဒီလမ်းက လာခဲ့ပါ။

Alright, Mr. Noto.
Kyaung bar byi Mr. Noto.
ကောင်းပါပြီ မစ္စတာ နိတို။

Here we are! Won't you sit down? I will find the dictionary on the shelf.
Di mhar bar. Khinbya htaing bar. Kyundaw sin paw hmar abidan shar par ya say.
ဒီမှာပါ။ ခင်ဗျားထိုင်ပါ။ ကျွန်တော် စင်ပေါ်မှာ အဘိဓာန် ရှာပါရစေ။

Thank you, Mr. Noto. I really do not like borrowing books from somebody but I must have an English dictionary this evening.
Kyawzu tin bar dae Mr. Noto. Kyundaw thu mya si ga saroke ma hnar gyin bar bu khinbya. Dar bae mae di nya nay abidan go ayay ta gyi lo ut nay bar dae.
ကျေးဇူးတင်ပါတယ် မစ္စတာ နိတို။ ကျွန်တော် သူများဆီက စာအုပ်မငှားချင်ပါဘူးခင်ဗျား။ ဒါပေမယ့် ဒီညနေ အဘိဓာန် ကို အရေးတကြီးလိုအပ်နေပါတယ်။

Is it here in the bottom shelf?
Abidan ga di sar ouk sin out phat mhar lar.
အဘိဓာန်က ဒီစာအုပ်စင်အောက်ဖက်မှာလား။

No, it is not here.
Ma hoke par bu. Di mhar ma shi bu.
မဟုတ်ပါဘူး။ ဒီမှာ မရှိဘူး။

Oh, don't worry. Mr. Noto, if you can't find it.
O khinbya shar ma twe gae yin seik ma pu bar nae Mr. Noto.
အို ခင်ဗျား ရှာမတွေ့ခဲ့ရင် စိတ်မပူပါနဲ့ မစ္စတာ နိုတို။

It seems that I have to wait till tomorrow, when I can buy one.
*Kyi ya dar kyundaw manet phyan wae loe ya dae achain go sauk
ya mae nae tu dae.*
ကြည့်ရတာ ကျွန်တော် မနက်ဖြန် ဝယ်လို့ရတဲ့ အချိန်ကို
စောင့်ရမယ်နဲ့တူတယ်။

It must be somewhere on the shelves. Here it is on the shelf!
*Sar ouk sin yae`. tiq nay yar hmar shi ya hmar par. Di mhar ae`
da sar ouk sin paw mhar bar.*
စာအုပ်စင်ရဲ့ တစ်နေရာမှာ ရှိရမှာပါ။ ဒီမှာ အဲဒါ စာအုပ်စင်ပေါ်မှာ ပါ။

I do not know who has placed it here. I always put it on the
bottom shelf.
*Bae thu nayar pyaung htar tha lae kyundaw mathi bu. Kyundaw
ga amyae sar ouk sin yae auk phat mhar hatar dar go.*
ဘယ်သူ နေရာပြောင်းထားသလဲ ကျွန်တော်မသိဘူး။ ကျွန်တော်က
အမြဲ စာအုပ်စင်ရဲ့ အောက်ဖက်မှာ ထားတာကိုး။

Here you are!
Di mhar bar khinbya.
ဒီမှာ ပါခင်ဗျား။

Thank you, Mr. Noto. This is what I want. I need it very much.
Kyaezu tin bar dae Mr. Noto. Di har kyundaw loe gyin dae har bar. Kyundaw alun loe ut nay dar bar.
ကျေးဇူးတင်ပါတယ် မစ္စတာ နိုတို။ ဒီဟာ ကျွန်တော်လိုချင်တဲ့ဟာပါ။ ကျွန်တော်အလွန်လိုအပ်နေတာပါ။

It has been a pleasure, Mr. Harun. Don't worry about it.
Di kate sa ga wun thar sa yar bar Mr. Harun. Seik ma pu bar nae.
ဒီကိစ္စက ဝမ်းသာစရာပါ မစ္စတာဟာရွန်။ စိတ်မပူပါနဲ့။

I think it is time for me to go now. I hope you will not be offended.
May I be excused?
Kyundaw go thwa khwint pyu bar khinbya. Khinbya seik ma soe bu loe kyundaw mhaw lin bar dae. Khwint pyu par khinbya.
ကျွန်တော် ကို သွားခွင့်ပြုပါခင်ဗျား။ ခင်ဗျား စိတ်မဆိုးဘူးလို့ ကျွန်တော် မျှော်လင့်ပါတယ်။ ခွင့်ပြုပါ ခင်ဗျား။

Do you need to go back so soon? Can't you stay a little longer?
Khinbya ayay ta gyi pyan phoe loe nay tha lar. Di mhar nay loe ya thay tha lar.
ခင်ဗျား အရေးတကြီး ပြန်ဖို့လိုနေသလား။ ဒီမှာ နေလို့ရသေးသလား။

I wish I could. But I have some homework to do. And I do not want to waste your time.
Kyundaw nay gyin bar dae. Dar pay mae Kyundaw hmar aloke twe shi nay loe bar. Nauk pyi Kyundaw khinbya yae achain dwe go ma phyone tee gyin bar bu.
ကျွန်တော် နေချင်ပါတယ်။ ဒါပေမယ့်ကျွန်တော့်မှာ အလုပ်တွေရှိနေလို့ပါ။ နောက်ပြီး ကျွန်တော် ခင်ဗျားရဲ့အချိန်တွေကို မဖြုန်းတီးချင်ပါဘူး။

Well, I cannot keep you, then. Come again when you have time.
Give my regards to your family.

Kaung bar byi. Khinbya thwa bar. Khinbya hmar achain ya yin
nauk lae lar gae bar. Khinbya mithasu atwet su taung myita pay
like par ya say.

ကောင်းပါပြီ၊ ခင်ဗျားသွားပါ။ ခင်ဗျားမှာ အချိန်ရရင် နောက်လည်း
လာခဲ့ပါ။ ခင်ဗျားမိသားစု အတွက် ဆုတောင်းမေတ္တာ ပေးလိုက်ပါ
ရစေ။

Natural World
Tha-bar-wa Kaba
သဘာဝကမ္ဘာ။

Air
Lay
လေ

Cloud
Moh: dayn
မိုးတိမ်

Cold
Ay-jin:, ah-ay:
အေးခြင်း၊ အအေး

Comet
Kyeh-teh-goon
ကြယ်တံခွန်

Darkness
Mhaung mik-chin:
မှောင်မိုက်ခြင်း

Dew/Fog
Hnin:/See:-hnin:
နှင်း၊ ဆီးနှင်း

Dust
Ah-hmohn, hpohk
အမှုန်၊ ဖုတ်

Earth
Myay, myay-jee
မြေ။ မြေကြီး

Earthquake
Myay nga hlin hloke chin
မြေငလျင်လှုပ်ခြင်း

East
Ah-shay. Ayat
အရှေ့အရပ်

Eclipse (of sun)
Nay-kyaht-chin
နေကြတ်ခြင်း

Fire
Mee:
မီး

Frost
See:-hnin-geh
ဆီးနှင်းခဲ

Heat
Ah-poo
အပူ

Light
A-lin
အလင်း

Moon
Lah
လ

North
Myowk a yut
မြောက်အရပ်

Rain
Moh: yooah jin:
မိုးရွာခြင်း

Thunder
Moh:-chohn:-jin
မိုးခြိုးခြင်း

Weather
Moh:-lay watha
မိုးလေဝသ

Wind
Lay-tik-chin:
လေတိုက်ခြင်း

Fruits, Trees, Flowers And Vegetables
Apin, Athi, Pan A Myo: Myo:
အပင်၊အသီး၊ ပန်းအမျိုးမျိုး။

Almond
Bh-dahn
ဗါဒါန်

Asparagus
Kah-nyoot
ကညွတ်

Banana
Hgnet-pyaw
ငှက်ပျော

Beans
Pea
ပဲ

Cabbage
Gaw-phee
ဂေါ်ဖီ

Carrot
Mon-lah-oo-war
မုံလာဥဝါ

Coconut
Ohn:
အုန်း

Cucumber
Thah-hkwah:
သခွား

Durian
Doo:-yin:
ဒူးရင်း

Garlic
Kyet-thoon-phyu
ကြက်သွန်ဖြူ

Grape
Zahpyit
စပျစ်

Lemon
Showk-chin
ရှောက်ချဉ်

Lime
Thahmbahyah
သံပုရာ

Maize
Pyaung-phoo
ပြောင်းဖူး

Mango
Thah-yet
သရက်

Mushroom
Hmoh
မှို

Onion
Kyet-thoon-nee
ကြက်သွန်နီ

Papaya
Thin-baw-thee
သင်္ဘောသီး

Pepper
Nga-yoke-kaung
ငရုတ်ကောင်း

Pineapple
Nanat
နာနတ်

Plum
Zee-thee
ဇီးသီး

Tamarind
Ma-jee:
မန်ကျည်း

Tomato
Kha-yan-chin-thee
ခရမ်းချဉ်သီး

Mesua ferrea flower
Kankaw pann
ကံကော်ပန်း။

Lotus flower
Kyar pann
ကြာပန်း။

Star flower
Kha yay pann
ခရေပန်း။

Cherry flower
Cherry pann
ချယ်ရီပန်း။

Jasmine flower
Zabe` pann
စံပယ်ပန်း။

Laburnum flower
Ngu war pann
ငုဝါပန်း။

Gum-kino flower
Ba dauk pann
ပိတောက်ပန်း။

Orchid flower
Thit khwa pann
သစ်ခွပန်း။

Aster flower
May myot pann
မေမြို့ပန်း။

Rose flower
Hninn ze pann
နှင်းဆီပန်း။

Dimension
Atai-atar
အတိုင်းအတာ။

Length
Alya:; a shei
အလျား၊ အရှည်

Breadth
Anan; akye
အနံ၊ အကျယ်

Height
Amyin
အမြင့်

Thickness
Ahtu; du.
အထူ၊ ထု

Depth
Ane', zau'
အနက်၊ ဇောက်

Holidays In Myanmar
Ar-lat-yet-myar:
အားလပ်ရက်များ။

Western calendar holidays in Myanmar are:

Independence Day (4th January)
Lut-la-yay-nay.
လွတ်လပ်ရေးနေ့.

Union (12th February)
Pyi-htaung-zu-nay.
ပြည်ထောင်စုနေ့.

Peasants' Day (2nd March)
Taung-thu-lae-tha-mar-nay.
တောင်သူလယ်သမားနေ့.

Army Day (27 March)
Ta-ma-daw-nay.
တပ်မတော်နေ့.

Workers' Day (1st May)
A-louk-tha-ma-nay.
အလုပ်သမားနေ့.

Martyrs' Day (19th July)
A-zar-ni-nay.
အာဇာနည်နေ့.

Christmas Day (25th December)
Khrisamapwedawnay.
ခရစ်စမတ်ပွဲတော်နေ့.

Karen New Year (1st of Pya-dhou)
Kyin-hnit-thit-ku-nay.
ကရင်နှစ်သစ်ကူးနေ့.

Full moon of tabaung
Ta-baung-pwe-daw-nay.
တပေါင်းပွဲတော်နေ့.

Water Festival (4 days in early tagu)
Thin-gyan
သင်္ကြန်

Buddha Festival (full moon of Ka-son)
Nyaung-ye-thun-pwe-daw
ညောင်ရေသွန်းပွဲတော်

Buddhist lent begins (full moon of Waso)
Da-ma-se-kyar-nay.
ဓမ္မစကြာနေ့.

End of Lent (full moon of Tha-din-gyut)
A-bi-da-ma-nay.
အဘိဓမ္မာနေ့.

Festival of Lights (full moon of Ta-zun-daing)
Ta-zaun-daing-pwe-daw
တန်ဆောင်တိုင်ပွဲတော်

National Day (10th waning of Ta-zun-mon)
Amyo-tha-nay.
အမျိုးသားနေ့.

Arrival At The Airport
Lay Seik Ko Saik Yauk Chin:
လေဆိပ်ကို ဆိုက်ရောက်ခြင်း॥

Q: Show me your passport, please.
Pas-sa-po pya ba, khin bya.
ပါတ်စပုတ် ပြပါခင်ဗျား॥

A: Here is my passport.
Pas-sa-po di hma.
ပါစပုတ် ဒီမှာ॥

Q: How long are you going to stay?
Be lauk kya kya nay hma le:?
ဘယ်လောက်ကြာကြာနေမှာလဲ॥

A: Just one or two days.
Tayet hnityet lauk pa.
တစ်ရက်၊ နှစ်ရက်လောက်ပါ॥

> A week
> *Da pat*
> တစ်ပတ်॥
>
> Two weeks
> *Hnit pat*
> နှစ်ပတ်॥
>
> A month
> *Ta la*
> တစ်လ॥

Q: Where are you going to stay?
Bei hma nay hma le:?
ဘယ်မှာ နေမှာလဲ။

A: I will stay in one of the hotels.
Hote`ta khu khu hma nay mai`
ဟိုတယ်တစ်ခုခုမှာ နေမယ်။

President Hotel
Tamada Hote`
သမ္မတ ဟိုတယ်။

Inya Lake Hotel
Inya Leik Hote`
အင်းလျားလိပ် ဟိုတယ်။

Strand Hotel
Kan Na: Hote`
ကန်းနား ဟိုတယ်။

Karaweik Hotel
Karaweik Hote`
ကရဝိတ် ဟိုတယ်။

Trader's Hotel
Trader Hote`
ထရေးဒါး ဟိုတယ်။

Sedona Hotel
Sedona Hote`
စီဒိုးနား ဟိုတယ်။

A: I will stay at a friend's house.
A-thi. tayauk ein hma nay me`.
အသိတစ်ယောက် အိမ်မှာ နေမယ်။

Q: Tell me the address.
Lei`-sar pyaw ba.
လိပ်စာ ပြောပါ။

A: No. 20, Yaw-min-gyi Street, Yangon.
Amhat nnit se, yaw-min-gyi lan, Yangon.
အမှတ်–၂၀ ယောမင်းကြီးလမ်း၊ ရန်ကုန်မြို့။

Q: What is the reason for coming?
Ba akyaun: ne` la da le:?
ဘာ အကြောင်းနဲ့ လာတာလဲ။

A: On a holiday.
A-le` lar da bar.
အလည်လာတာပါ။

On a business trip.
A-louk ne` lar da bar.
အလုပ်နဲ့ လာတာပါ။

On a field trip.
Lay` la ye: kha yee twet la da bar.
လေ့လာရေး ခရီးထွက်လာတာပါ။

Q: What is your occupation?
Bar a louk louk the le:?
ဘာအလုပ်လုပ် သလဲ။

A: I am a student.
Kyunaw Kyaun tha ta yauk pa
ကျွန်တော်ကျောင်းသားတစ်ယောက်ပါ။

I am a teacher.
Kyunaw sayar ta yauk pa.
ကျွန်တော် ဆရာတစ်ယောက်ပါ။

I am a businessman.

Kyunaw Kon The ta yauk pa.

ကျွန်တော်ကုန်သည်တစ်ယောက်ပါ ။

Okay, you can take back your passport.

Kaun bi, khin mya pas-pot pyan yu naing bi.

ကောင်းပြီ၊ပါ.စပုတ်ပြန်ယူနိုင်ပြီ ။

Thank you.

Kyei: zu tin bar de` khamya.

ကျေးဇူးတင်ပါတယ် ခင်ဗျား ။

Authority
Anar-paing-aphwe-ase
အာဏာပိုင်အဖွဲ့အစည်း။

Administration
Oh cho yey
အုပ်ချုပ်ရေး

Prime Minister
Wan-jee cho
ဝန်ကြီးချုပ်

President
Tha-ma-da
သမ္မတ

Vice President
Du-te-ya tha-ma-da
ဒုတိယ သမ္မတ

Military
Tatmadaw
တပ်မတော်

Chairman
Oh-ga-hta
ဥက္ကဋ္ဌ

Parliament
Hluttaw
လွှတ်တော်

Politics
Nine-ngan-yey
နိုင်ငံရေး

Accommodation
Nayar-htaing-khin Myar:
နေရာထိုင်ခင်းများ။

To Stay
Nayan
နေရန်

Bed
Ga din
ကုတင်

Restroom
Ehn tha
အိမ်သာ

Shower
Yay cho khan
ရေချိုးခန်း

Bathtub
Yei-cho-gan
ရေချိုးကန်

Blanket
Saun
စောင်

Candle
Pha-yaun-dain
ဖယောင်းတိုင်

Clean
Than' (de`)/Shin (de`)
သန့်ရှင်းတယ်

Dinner
Nya-za
ညစာ

Dirty
Nyi'-pa' (te)
ညစ်ပတ်တယ်

Door
Da-ga
တံခါး

Fan (electric)
Pan-ka
ပန်ကာ

Key
Tho'
သော့

Lock
Tho'-ga-lau
သော့ခလောက်

Lunch
Nei-le-za
နေ့လည်စာ

Noisy
Na`-nyi (de)
နားညီးတယ်

Pillow
(Ga`un)o`un
ခေါင်းအုံး

Quiet
Tei' (te)
တိတ်တယ်

Roof
Amo`u
အမိုး

Sheet
Hcounzaun/Ei'yahkin
ခြုံစောင်၊ အိပ်ရာခင်း

Shower
Yei-ban
ရေပန်း

Sleep
Ei'(te)
အိပ်တယ်

Soap
Sa'pya
ဆပ်ပြာ

Suitcase/Box
Tei'ta
သေတ္တာ

Tap
Yei-htwe'pau'
ရေထွက်ပေါက်

Towel
Mye'hna thou' hpawa
မျက်နှာသုတ်ပုဝါ

Wash (body)
Yei hco`u (de)
ရေချိုးတယ်

Wash (clothes)
A 'wu' sho (de)
အဝတ်လျှော်တယ်

Wash (hair)
Ga`un sho (de)
ခေါင်းလျှော်တယ်

Window
Pya 'dinbau'
ပြူတင်းပေါက်

Booking A Room At A Hotel
Hote` Ta Khu Hma A Khan Hnar Chin:
ဟိုတယ်တစ်ခုမှာ အခန်းငှားခြင်း

I want a room.
A khan ta khan lo chin de`.
အခန်း တစ်ခန်း လိုချင်တယ်။

Single room or double room?
Ta yauk khan lar, hnit yauk khan lar?
တစ်ယောက်ခန်းလား၊ နှစ်ယောက်ခန်းလား။

Single room. How much is one night?
Ta yauk khan bar. Ta nya go bei lauk le`?
တစ်ယောက်ခန်းပါ၊ တစ်ညကို ဘယ်လောက်လဲ။

One night is 300 kyats.
Ta nya go kyat tone yar bar.
တစ်ညကို ကျပ် သုံးရာ ပါ။

Have an air-con?
Lay ee: set par ta lar:?
လေအေးစက်ပါ သလား။

Have
Par bar de`
ပါပါတယ်။

Have TV and refrigerator?
TV, ye-ge`te-tar par da lar?
တီဗီ၊ ရေခဲ သေတ္တာ ပါသလား၊

Okay, I'll take it.
Kaun bi, Kyunaw yu me.
ကောင်းပြီ။ ကျွန်တော်ယူမယ်။

Here's the key.
Di hma tau`
ဒီမှာ သော့။

Thank you
Kye-zu-tin ba de`.
ကျေးဇူးတင်ပါတယ်။

Don't mention it.
Kek-sa ma shi bar bu.
ကိစ္စ မရှိပါဘူး။

Leaving A Hotel
Hote Hma Hwet Khwar Gyin
ဟိုတယ်မှ ထွက်ခွါခြင်း

Here is your laundry, sir!
Di mya khin bya ye`. a wutwe par saya.
ဒီမှာ ခင်ဗျားရဲ့ အဝတ်တွေပါ။ ဆရာ။

Two white and two coloured shirts. Five handkerchiefs and two
pairs of nylon stockings.
*Aphyu hint hte nae ayaun shart ingyi hnit hte bar. lakai puwar
nga hte nae chae eik hnit sone bar.*
အဖြူ နှစ်ထည် နဲ့ အရောင်ရုပ်အကျီ နှစ်ထည်ပါ။
လက်ကိုင်ပုဝါငါးထည် နဲ့ ခြေအိပ် နှစ်စုံပါ။

How much is it?
Di har be lauk le`?
ဒီဟာ ဘယ်လောက်လဲ။

Five hundred and twenty kyats, sir.
Nga ya nae hnit se kyat bar saya.
ငါးရာ နဲ့ နှစ်ဆယ် ကျပ်ပါ။ ဆရာ။

Here you are! Will you carry these suitcases down to the office?
Di hma bar. khin bya eitwe go out htut yone khan go you thwa mha la:
ဒီမှာပါ။ ခင်ဗျား အိတ်တွေကို အောက်ထပ်ရုံးခန်းကို ယူသွားမှာ လား။

Certainly, sir. Are you going to leave?
Hoke par tae. saya. khin bya thwa daw. mae ma hoke la:?
ဟုတ်ပါတယ်။ ဆရာ။ ခင်ဗျား သွားတော့မယ်မဟုတ်လား။

Yes, I will get my things in. I am ready. Come, let us go.
Hoke par tae. kyun daw pitsae dwe thein like par mae. asin thin par. thwa gya soe.
ဟုတ်ပါတယ်။ ကျွန်တော် ပစ္စည်းတွေ သိမ်းလိုက်ပါမယ်.
အဆင်သင့်ပါ။ သွားကြစို့.။

At the Office
Yone khan mha
ရုံးခန်းမှာ

May I have the bill, please?
Kyaezu pyut pyi kya thin nge sayin pay par khin bya?
ကျေးဇူးပြုပြီး ကျသင့်ငွေစာရင်း ပေးပါခင်ဗျား။

Room number forty-five.
Akhan nanbat ngasae ga par khin bya.
အခန်းနံပါတ် ငါးဆယ်ကပါ ခင်ဗျား။

A few seconds, please.
Khana sau. par khin bya.
ခဏစောင့်ပါ ခင်ဗျာ။

All right. I can wait.
Kuan: ba byi. sau. naing par tae.
ကောင်းပါပြီ။ စောင့်နိုင်ပါတယ်။

Here is your bill, sir! Eight thousand two hundred and fifty Kyats.
Dimha khin bya kya thin nge sayin par saya. shithaung hnitya ngasae kyat par.
ဒီမှာ ခင်ဗျား ကျသင့်ငွေစာရင်းပါ ဆရာ။ ရှစ်ထောင် နှစ်ရာ ငါးဆယ်
ကျပ် ပါ။

Here is money!
Di mha ngwe bar.
ဒီမှာ ငွေပါ။

Have you been very comfortable here, sir?
Di mha saya nae htwe ya da asin pyayae la: khin bya?
ဒီမှာ ဆရာ နေထိုင်ရတာ အဆင်ပြေရဲ့လားခင်ဗျာ ။

Sure, I am very comfortable.
Hoke par dae. asin pyay bar dae.
ဟုတ်ပါတယ်။ အဆင်ပြေပါတယ်။

I hope you will come again, sir. Do you want a taxi? The hall-
porter will get you one.
*Nauk tiq khar la gae par kiin bya. anga yin alo shi par da la: won
htan tiq oo ga si sin pay par lake mae.*
နောက်တစ်ခါလာခဲ့ပါခင်ဗျား။ အငှားယာဉ် အလိုရှိပါသလား။
ဝန်ထမ်းတစ်ဦး က စီစဉ်ပေးပါလိမ့်မယ်။

Yes, I do. I want to go to Yangon International airport.
Hoke par dae. kyun daw yangon lae seik go thwa gin par dae.
ဟုတ်ပါတယ်။ ကျွန်တော် ရန်ကုန်လေဆိပ်ကို သွားချင်ပါတယ်။

The taxi is here, sir. Shall I take your cases into the taxi?
*Di mha anga yin par. kyun daw doe pitsae dwe anga yin hte go po
pay par ya sae?*
ဒီမှာ အငှားယာဉ်ပါ။ ကျွန်တော်တို့ ပစ္စည်းတွေ အငှားယာဉ် ထဲကို
ပို့ပေးပါရစေ။

144

At The Seaside

Pin Lae Kan Chae Mhar

ပင်လယ်ကမ်းခြေမှာ

Is there a good sea-beach around here?
Di ani anar mhar hla pa tae kan chae tiq khu lauk shi tha lar?
ဒီအနီးအနားမှာ လှပတဲ့ကမ်းခြေတစ်ခုလောက်ရှိသလား။

Yes, there is one at Ngwe Saung.
Shi bar dae. Ngwe Saung kan chae shi bar dae.
ရှိပါတယ်။ ငွေဆောင်ကမ်းခြေ ရှိပါတယ်။

How far is it from here?
Di ga nae bae lauk way bar tha lae?
ဒီကနေ ဘယ်လောက်ဝေးပါသလဲ။

It will take about an hour by car.
Car nae soe yin tiq nar yi lauk thaw ya bar lake mae.
ကားနဲ့ဆိုရင် တစ်နာရီလောက်သွားရပါလိမ့်မယ်။

You can go to Ngwe Saung by bus.
Khinbya Ngwe Saung go bus car nae lae thaw loe ya bar dae.
ခင်ဗျား ငွေဆောင်ကို ဘတ်စ်ကားနဲ့လည်း သွားလို့ရပါတယ်။

I like swimming.
Kyundaw yae ku ya da go kyaik tae.
ကျွန်တော် ရေကူးရတာကို ကြိုက်တယ်။

Let's go for a swim.
Yae ku pho thwa gya soe.
ရေကူးဖို့သွားကြစို့။

Where can I buy a bathing suit?
Yae ku wut sone tiq khu bae mhar wae loe ya bar ma lae khinbya?
ရေကူးဝတ်စုံတစ်ခု ဘယ်မှာ ဝယ်လို့ရပါမလဲခင်ဗျား။

From one of the fancy goods stores.
Fancy pyit si dwe yaung dae sai dwe mhar ya naing par de`.
ဖင်န်စီ ပစ္စည်းတွေ ရောင်းတဲ့ဆိုင်တွေမှာ ရနိုင်ပါတယ်။

I like to walk along the beach at low tide.
Di yae kya chein mhar kyundaw kan chae tiq hlauk lan chlauk chin bar dae.
ဒီရေကျချိန်မှာ ကျွန်တော် ကမ်းခြေတစ်လျှောက်လမ်း လျှောက်ချင်ပါ တယ်။

Swimming will improve your muscle tone.
Yae ku chin har kwetha dwe go toe tat lar say bar dae.
ရေကူးခြင်းဟာ ကြွက်သားတွေကို တိုးတက်လာစေပါတယ်။

What a lovely beach.
O bae lauk hla pa dae kan chae bar lake.
အိုး၊ ဘယ်လောက်လှပတဲ့ကမ်းခြေပါလိမ့်။

I have a pain in my back.
Kyundaw mhar khar nar yaw gar shi dae.
ကျွန်တော်မှာ ခါးနာရောဂါ ရှိတယ်။

We will stay half an hour in the water.
Kyundaw doe yae htae mhar nar yi wet lauk nay kya mae naw.
ကျွန်တော်တို့ ရေထဲမှာ နာရီဝက်လောက် နေကြမယ်နော်။

After that let us sunbathe on the beach.
A` da pyi yin nae pu mhar achaukhan kya mae.
အဲဒါပြီးရင်၊ နေပူမှာ အခြောက်ခံကြမယ်။

You swim very well.
Khinbya yae ku theik taw dae.
ခင်ဗျား ရေကူးသိပ်တော်တယ်။

I name you Queen of the South Sea.
Kyundaw khinbya go taung phet pin lae yae`. bayinma loe. bae khaw daw. mae.
ကျွန်တော် ခင်ဗျားကို တောင်ဖက်ပင်လယ်ရဲ့ဘုရင်မ
လို့ဘဲခေါ်တော့မယ်။

It is almost one o' clock now.
Akhu nae lae tiq naryi taung shi taw. mae.
အခု နေ့လည်တစ်နာရီတောင် ရှိတော့မယ်။

The tide has gone down.
Di yae kya taw. mae.
ဒီရေကျတော့မယ်။

We better get dressed for lunch.
Kyundaw doe nae lae sar sar: pho awut lae kya yin kaung mae.
ကျွန်တော်တို့ နေ့လည်စာစားဖို့ အဝတ်လဲကြရင်ကောင်းမယ်။

Let's go to an eating shop.

Sar: thauk sai tiq khu khu go thwa kya soe.

စားသောက်ဆိုင် တစ်ခုခု ကို သွားကြစို့။

That is my car.

Di har kyundaw. kar.

ဒီဟာ ကျွန်တော့် ကား။

You're not hungry, are you?

Khinbya ma sar they: bu. Hoke tae ma hoke lar?

ခင်ဗျား မဆာသေးဘူး။ ဟုတ်တယ်မဟုတ်လား။

Here we are. The "Good Food" Restaurant.

Haw kyundaw doe di mhar. sar: thauk sai kaung tiq khu pau.

ဟော ကျွန်တော်တို့ဒီမှာ။ စားသောက်ဆိုင်ကောင်းတစ်ခုပေါ့။

The food is marvellous.

Asar asar: dwe ga taw antma khan lauk sayar bae.

အစားအစာတွေကတော့ အံ့မခန်းလောက်စရာဘဲ။

Thank you for bringing me here.

Kyundaw go di go khaw lar tae atwet kyae zu tin bar dae.

ကျွန်တော့်ကို ဒီကို ခေါ်လာတဲ့အတွက် ကျေးဇူးတင်ပါတယ်။

At A Clinic/Hospital

Thama Daw Tiq Oo Hnit Tawe Sone Chin.

သမားတော်တစ်ဦးနှင့် တွေ့ဆုံခြင်း။

What is the matter with you?

Khinbya bar mya phyt loe bar lake?

ခင်ဗျား ဘာများ ဖြစ်လို့ပါလိမ့်။

I don't feel well. I need a doctor.

Kyundaw nae ma kaung bu khinbya. Saya wun tiq oo oo nae twe bar ya sae.

ကျွန်တော်နေမကောင်းဘူးခင်ဗျား။ ဆရာဝန်တစ်ဦးဦးနဲ့တွေ့ပါရစေ။

Is there a drugstore near here?

Di anianar: mhar sae sai tiq khu shi da lar?

ဒီအနီးအနားမှာ ဆေးဆိုင်တစ်ခု ရှိသလား။

Where is the hospital?

Say: yong bae mhar shi tha lae`?

ဆေးရုံဘယ်မှာ ရှိသလဲ။

Please send me to a hospital.

Kyundaw go say: yong go khaw thwa bar.

ကျွန်တော့်ကို ဆေးရုံ ကို ခေါ်သွားပါ။

Call the ambulance, please.

Kyae zu pyu pyi, thunar tin yin khaw pay bar.

ကျေးဇူးပြုပြီး၊ သူနာတင်ယာဉ် ခေါ်ပေးပါ။

I have headache, pain in all my bones and joints.

Kyundaw khaung theik kite tae, ayo asit twe ar lone nar kyin nae bar dae.

ကျွန်တော် ခေါင်းသိပ်ကိုက်တယ်။ အရိုး၊ အဆစ်တွေ အားလုံးနာကျင်နေပါတယ်။

I have diarrhoea and gripping pains in the abdomen.

Kyundaw wan shaw pyi, wan bike atwin phat go soke swe hta tha lo nar kyin nae bar dae.

ကျွန်တော်ဝမ်းလျှောပြီး၊ ဝမ်းဗိုက်အတွင်းဖက်ကို ဆုပ်ဆွဲထားသလို နာကျင်နေပါတယ်။

Who is the best doctor in this place?

Di nae yar ta wite mhar akaung soe sayawun ga bae thu lae`?

ဒီနေရာတဝိုက်မှာ အကောင်းဆုံးဆရာဝန်က ဘယ်သူလဲ။

Is there a foreign doctor here?

Di nar mhar naing ngan char thar sayawun tiq oo lauk shit tha lar:?

ဒီနားမှာ နိုင်ငံခြားသား ဆရာဝန်တစ်ဦးလောက်ရှိသလား။

Where does he live?

Thu bae mhar nae bar tha lae`?

သူဘယ်မှာ နေပါသလဲ။

Will you send me to him immediately, as I feel quite ill.

Khinbya kyndaw. go thu si go amyan sone poe pay naing bar tha lar? Kyundaw ataw. go phya nae bar byi.

ခင်ဗျားကျွန်တော့်ကို သူ့ဆီကို အမြန်ဆုံးပို့ပေးနိုင်ပါသလား။ ကျွန်တော် အတော့်ကို ဖျားနေပါပြီ။

I don't feel very well, doctor.
Doctor, kyundaw nae ma kaung bar bu khinbya.
ဒေါက်တာ၊ ကျွန်တော် နေမကောင်းပါဘူး ခင်ဗျား။

What seems to be the trouble?
Bae lo waidanar myo khan sar nae ya bar tha lae`?
ဘယ်လိုဝေဒနာမျိုးခံစားနေရပါသလဲ။

I suffer from sleeplessness.
Kyundaw eik yay maya tae`. Waidanar khan sar: nay ya bar dae.
ကျွန်တော် အိပ်ရေးမဝတဲ့ဝေဒနာ ခံစားနေရပါတယ်။

I feel a little tired.
Kyundaw nae nae pin pan nae bar dae.
ကျွန်တော် နည်းနည်း ပင်ပန်းနေပါတယ်။

I also have some pain occasionally.
Kyundaw ta khar ta yan nar kyin mhyu go khan zar: ya bar dae.
ကျွန်တော် တစ်ခါတရံ နာကျင်မှုကို ခံစားရပါတယ်။

It might be ....
.... *Phyit naing bar dae.*
.... ဖြစ်နိုင်ပါတယ်။

> Rheumatism
> *Asit amyit kite khae dae waidanar*
> အဆစ်အမြစ်ကိုက်ခဲတဲ့ ဝေဒနာ
>
> Neuritis
> *Aryong gyaw yaund dae waidanar*
> အာရုံကြောရောင်တဲ့ဝေဒနာ

Arthritis
Asit amyit yaung dae waidanar
အဆစ်အမြစ်ရောင်တဲ့ဝေဒနာ

Poor circulation
Thwe hlate pat mhu nhye kwye dae waidanar
သွေးလှည့်ပတ်မှု နေးကွေးတဲ့ ဝေဒနာ

Kidney trouble
Kyaukat yawgar waidanar
ကျောက်ကပ်ရောဂါ ဝေဒနာ

Heart trouble
Athe yawgar waidanar
အသည်းရောဂါ ဝေဒနာ

How is your appetite?
Khinbya sar: thauk chin seik shi thae tha lar?
ခင်ဗျား စားသောက်ချင်စိတ်ရှိသေးသလား။

I have hardly eaten anything these two days.
Kyundaw asar:athauk pyat nay dar hnit yet shi bar byi.
ကျွန်တော် အစားအသောက်ပျက်နေတာ နှစ်ရက်ရှိပါပြီ။

I am suffering from constipation.
Kyundaw wan chauk nay bar dae.
ကျွန်တော် ဝမ်းချုပ်နေပါတယ်။

I have rheumatic pains in my joints.
Kyundaw asit amyit kite khae dae waidanar khan zar: nae ya bar dae.
ကျွန်တော် အဆစ်အမြစ်ကိုက်ခဲတဲ့ ဝေဒနာခံစားနေရပါတယ်။

152

Where do you feel pain now?
Akhu gaw bae nayar mhar narkyin nay bar tha lae?
အခုကော ဘယ်နေရာမှာ နာကျင်နေပါသလဲ။

I have a pain here.
Di nayar mhar narkyin nay bar dae.
ဒီနေရာမှာ နာကျင်နေပါတယ်။

Do you have a pain in your chest?
Khinbya yinbat mhar narkyin nay bar tha lar?
ခင်ဗျား ရင်ဘတ်မှာ နာကျင်နေပါသလား။

I have a stabbing pain in the side and cannot lie down.
Kyundaw khandar koe bay bat twe har narkyin nay loe le lyaung loe ma ya bar bu.
ကျွန်တော် ခန္ဓာကိုယ်ဘေးဘက်တွေဟာ နာကျင်နေလို့
လဲလျောင်းလို့မရပါဘူး။

Let me examine your chest.
Khinbya yinbat go sitsay kwint pyu bar.
ခင်ဗျား ရင်ဘတ်ကို စစ်ဆေးခွင့်ပြုပါ။

How long have you felt ill?
Di waidanar khan zar: nay dar bae laukyar bar byi le`?
ဒီဝေဒနာခံစားနေတာဘယ်လောက်ကြာပါပြီလဲ။

It began the day before yesterday by a shivering fit.
Ta myan nay. ga te ga tong khar pyi sa khae`. dar bar.
တစ်မြန်နေ့ကတည်းက တုန်ခါပြီး စခဲ့တာပါ။

You must have an injection to protect it.

Khinbay di waidanar go kar kwe phoe say ta loe htoe ya lake mae.

ခင်ဗျား ဒီဝေဒနာကို ကာကွယ်ဖို့ဆေးတစ်လုံးထိုးရလိမ့်မယ်॥

Do you think my illness dangerous?

Di waidanar har soe yeik ya tae waidanar loe khinbya htin bar tha lar?

ဒီဝေဒနာဟာ စိုးရိမ်ရတဲ့ ဝေဒနာလို့ ခင်ဗျား ထင်ပါသလား॥

If you take care of yourself, you will feel better soon.

Khinbya kaung kaung ga yu seik mae soe yin, ma kyar khin pyan lae kaung mon lar bar lake mae.

ခင်ဗျား ကောင်းကောင်းဂရုစိုက်မယ်ဆိုရင်၊ မကြာခင် ပြန်လည်ကောင်းမွန် လာပါ လိမ့်မယ်॥

Here are some pills.

Di mhar say a cho. Khinbya atwet par.

ဒီမှာ ဆေးအချို့ခင်ဗျားအတွက်ပါ॥

In two or three days you will be quite well.

Khinbya hnit yet, thone yet atwin kaung mon lar bar lake mae.

ခင်ဗျား နှစ်ရက်၊ သုံးရက်အတွင်း ကောင်းမွန်လာပါလိမ့်မယ်॥

Driving
Yin-maung-chin
ယာဉ်မောင်းခြင်း။

Car
Ka
ကား

Stop
Yet/Ho
ရပ်၊ ဟို;

Go/Drive
Thwa/Moun
သွား၊ မောင်း

Traffic Light
Mee point
မီးပွိုင့်.

Directions
Lan-hnyun
လမ်းညွှန်။

Over there
Ho beht
ဟိုဘက်

Right side
Nyabet
ညာဘက်

Turn please
Hleba
လှည့်.ပါ

Turn right please
Nyabet hleba
ညာဘက်လှည့်.ပါ

Left side
Bebet
ဘယ်ဘက်

Turn left please
Bebet hleba
ဘယ်ဘက်လှည့်.ပါ

On the right side
Nyabet hma
ညာဘက်မှာ

Exists
Shide
ရှိတယ်

There's (one) on the right
Nyabet hma shide
ညာဖက်မှာရှိတယ်

There's (one) on the left
Bebet hma shide
ဘယ်ဘက်မှာရှိတယ်

Straight ahead
Tede
တည့်.တည့်.

Go, please
Thaw ba
သွားပါ

Go straight ahead please
Tede thaw ba
တည့်.တည့်.သွားပါ

Here
Dihma
ဒီမှာ

It's here
Dihma shide
ဒီမှာ ရှိတယ်

Please point
Pya ba
ပြပါ

Asking For Directions

Lan Hnyun Pya Pay Yan May:
Myan Sone San Chin:

လမ်းညွှန်ပြပေးရန် စုံစမ်းမေးမြန်းခြင်း။

When did you arrive in this town?
"Bae done ga di myo go yauk tha lae?"
I arrived on Friday.
"Thaukya nae ga yauk par tae"
When will you go back?
"Bae daw. lauk pyan ma lae?"
I will go back on next Monday.
"Larmae taninlar nae pyan bar mae"
Can't you stay longer?
"Kyar kyar ma nay daw. bu lar?"
I can't.
"Ma nae daw. bar bu"

Can you tell me which way is ....?
.... *Go be ga twa ya the le`*
.... ကို ဘယ်ကသွားရသလဲ။

> Airport
> *Lay Zeit*
> လေဆိပ်

> Railway station
> *Buda Yon*
> ဘူတာရုံ

> Bus station
> *Basaka Gate*
> ဘတ်စ်ကားဂိတ်

> Market
> *Ze`*
> ဈေး

> School
> *Kyaun*
> ကျောင်း

> University of Malaya
> *Malaya Tek-ka-do*
> မလားရား တက္ကသိုလ်

> Library
> *Sar Kyi` Teik*
> စာကြည့်တိုက်

Where is the ....?
.... *Bei hma shi the le`?*
.... ဘယ်မှာရှိသလဲ။

Muslim restaurant
Musalin Sar Touk Saing
မွတ်စလင် စားသောက်ဆိုင်။

Guest house
E Yeik Tha
ဧရိပ်သာ

Clinic
Say Gan
ဆေးခန်း

Bank
Ban
ဘဏ်

Post office
Sar Teik
စာတိုက်

Malaysian Embassy
Malaysha Tan Yone
မလေးရှား သံရုံး

National Museum
Amyotha Pya Teik
အမျိုးသားပြတိုက်

Bogyoke Market
Bogyoke Zay
ဗိုလ်ချုပ်ဈေး

Immigration Office
Lu Win Hmu` Kyi Kyat Ye Yone
လူဝင်မှု ကြီးကြပ်ရေး ရုံး။

Police Station
Ye`Sa Khan
ရဲစခန်း

Hospital
Say Yon
ဆေးရုံ

Shwe Dagon Pagoda
Shwe Dagon Phaya:
ရွှေတိဂုံ ဘုရား

Mosque
Pali Kyaun:
ဗလီကျောင်း

Zoo
Tareiksan Yon
တိရိစ္ဆာန်ရုံ

Is it far?
Wei ta lar:?
ဝေးသလား။

Can I walk there?
E: di go lan shauk twa lo ya tha lar:?
အဲဒီ ကို လမ်းလျှောက်သွားလို့ရသလား။

Can I go by bus?
Bus-sa-kar ne` twa lo ya tha lar:?
ဘတ်စ်ကားနဲ့ သွားလို့ရသလား ။

Places Of Interests
Seik Win Sar Phwe Yar Nae Yar Day Tha Mya:
စိတ်ဝင်စားဖွယ်ရာ နေရာ ဒေသများ။

In Yangon

Shwe Dagon Pagoda
Shwe Dagon Phaya:
ရွှေတိဂုံဘုရား

Sule Pagoda
Sule Phaya:
ဆူးလေဘုရား

Kaba Aye Pagoda
Kaba Aye Phaya:
ကမ္ဘာအေးဘုရား

Bogyoke Market
Bogyoke Ze`
ဗိုလ်ချုပ်ဈေး

Zoo
Tareiksan Yon
တိရိစ္ဆာန်ရုံ

National Museum
Ahmyotha Pya Teik
အမျိုးသားပြတိုက်

Defence Services Museum
Tat Madaw Pya Teik
တပ်မတော်ပြတိုက်

Lawkanat Art Gallery
Lawkanat Bagyi Pya Khan
လောကနတ်ပန်းချီပြခန်း

Martyr's Musoleum
Arzani Beikman
အာဇာနည်ဗိမာန်

Kandaw Gyi Lake
Kandaw Gyi
ကန်တော်ကြီး

Htauk Kyant World War 11 Memorial
Htau` Kyan. Sit Thin: Gyain:
ထောက်ကြံ့ စစ်သချိုင်း

In Mandalay

Mandalay Hill
Man:dalei: Taung
မန္တလေး တောင်

Mandalay Palace Museum
Man:dalei: nan: dwin: Pya Teik
မန္တလေးနန်းတွင်းပြတိုက်

Mahamuni Pagoda
Mahamuni. Phaya:
မဟာမြမုနိဘုရား

Kuthodaw Pagoda (with its hundreds of stone inscriptions)
Kuthodaw Phaya:
ကုသိုလ်တော်ဘုရား

Kyauktawgyi: Pagoda
Kyauktawgyi: Phaya:
ကျောက်တော်ကြီးဘုရား

Tapestry Industry
Shwe Gyido: Louk Ngan:
ရွှေချည်ထိုးလုပ်ငန်း

From Mandalay, visitors can take a ride to nearby towns such as Ava, Sagaing, Pyin Oo Lwin.

In Pagan

Ananda Pagoda
Ananda Phaya
အာနန္ဒာဘုရား

Pagan Museum
Bagan Pya Taik
ပုဂံပြတိုက်

Lacquerware Museum
Yun Htei Pya Taik
ယွန်းထည်ပြတိုက်

Shwezigon Pagoda
Shwezigon Phaya
ရွှေစည်းခုံဘုရား

Thatbyinyu Pagoda
Thatbyinyu Phaya
သဗြင်းယုဘုရား

Sunset at Pagan is said to be breathtakingly beautiful and the most delightful moment one can experience in life. While in Pagan visitors can take time to visit Nyaung U and Poppa Hill.

Usage Of The Word 'WANT'
Chin De`
"ချင်တယ်" စကားလုံးအသုံးအနှုံး

I want to rent a taxi.
Kyunaw taxi ta si: hnga chin de`.
ကျွန်တော် တက်ကစီ တစ်စီးငှားချင်တယ်။

I want to eat rice.
Kyunaw htamin sar: chin de`.
ကျွန်တော် ထမင်းစားချင်တယ်။

I want to go to school.
Kyunaw kyaun thwa chin de`.
ကျွန်တော် ကျောင်းသွားချင်တယ်။

I want to see a picture (film).
Kyunaw yok shin kyi` chin de`.
ကျွန်တော် ရုပ်ရှင် ကြည်.ချင်တယ်။

I want to go sightseeing.
Kyunaw syauk lei chin de`.
ကျွန်တော် လျှောက်လည် ချင်တယ်။

I want to bathe.
Kyunaw ye cho chin de`.
ကျွန်တော် ရေချိုးချင်တယ်။

I want to study.

Kyunaw sar kyet chin de`.

ကျွန်တော် စာကျက်ချင်တယ်။

Telephone Conversation

Telephon Zagar Pyaw:

တယ်လီဖုံး စကားပြော။

"Hello. Who is it?"
"Akhu bae thu pyaw nay tha lae?"
"This is Maung Maung. Who is speaking?"
"Kyundaw Maung Maung bar?"
"I am Ma Thida."
"Kyunma Ma Thida bar"
"With whom do you want to speak?"
"Bathu nae pyaw chin bar tha lae?"
"May I speak with U Ba Mya?"
"Kyundaw U Ba Mya nae pyaw loe ya ma lar?"
"No, U Ba Mya is not here."
"U Ba Mya ma shi bar bu shin"

Ring...

Hello, who's there!
Hello bei tu le!
ဟဲလို ဘယ်သူလဲ။

Hello, I'm Azlan. Is Ali there?
Hello, kyunaw Azlan bar. Ali shi ta lar?
ဟဲလို.... ကျွန်တော် အဇ်လန်ပါ။ အလီ ရှိသလား။

He's in. Hold on for a moment
Shi bar de`. Khana kaing hta naw.
ရှိပါတယ်။ ခဏ ကိုင်ထားနော်။

Ali came...

Hello Azlan, how are you?
Hello Azlan... nay kaun lar`?
ဟဲလို အဇ်လန်... နေကောင်းလား။

I'm fine. Let's go sightseeing today.
Kaun ba de`. Di nay nga doe syauk lei ya aung.
ကောင်းပါတယ်။ ဒီနေ့ ငါတို့လျှောက်လည်ရအောင်။

Good idea. Where shall we go?
Kaun tha bei`. Ngadoe bei twa ja ma le`?
ကောင်းသားဘဲ။ ငါတို့ဘယ်သွားကြမလဲ။

We will go to KLCC. I will come after a moment.
KLCC go thwa me`. Kyunaw khana nay lar ge` me`.
KLCC ကို သွားမယ်။ ကျွန်တော်ခဏနေလာခဲ့မယ်။

170

Okay, I'll wait for you. See you.
Kaun bi, kyunaw saun` nay me`. Twe da pau`.
ကောင်းပြီ။ ကျွန်တော် စောင့်နေမယ်။ တွေ့တာပေါ့။

Okay.
Kaun bi.
ကောင်းပြီ။

"Is U Ba Mya there?"
"U Ba Mya shi bar tha lar"
"Where did he go?"
"Thu bae go thwa bar tha lae"
"I don't know."
"Ma thi bar bu shi"
"Then, who can I speak to?"
"Bathu go pyaw loe ya ma lae?"
"You can speak to me. I am his daughter."
"Kyunma go pyaw loe ya bar dae. Kyunma thu. thami bar"
"Please tell him that I cannot come today."
"Thu go pyaw bar. Di nae Kyunaw ma lar naing bar bu"
"Yes, I will tell my dad. Is that all?"
"Hokae, Kyunma aphay go pyaw bar me? Dar bae lar"
"Thank you. That's all."
"Hoke par dae. Dar bar bae"

171

Money Exchange
Ngwe Le`

ငွေလဲ

I want to change money.
Kyunaw ngwe le` chin de`.
ကျွန်တော် ငွေလဲချင်တယ်။

Is there a foreign money changer around here?
De nar hmar naing gan jar ngwe le` pay de` nay yar shi lar?
ဒီနားမှာ နိုင်ငံခြားငွေလဲပေးတဲ့ နေရာရှိသလား။

There is. On Shwe Bon Tar Street.
Shi bar de`. Shwe Bon Tar lan hma shi bar de`.
ရှိပါတယ်။ ရွှေဘုံသာလမ်းမှာ ရှိပါတယ်။

172

How much is the exchange rate?
Ngwe le`hnon: bai lauk le`?
ငွေလဲနှုန်း ဘယ်လောက်လဲ။

One American dollar is .... Kyats.
Ahmerican ta dollar go Myanmar ngwe .... kyat par
အမေရိကန် တစ်ဒေါ်လာကို မြန်မာငွေ .... ကျပ်ပါ။

Can you give me a better rate than that?
Ei di`hnon htat po pay naing ma lar:?
အဲဒီ နှုန်းထက်ပိုပေးနိုင်မလား။

No, I'm sorry. It is a fix rate.
Seik ma shi bar ne`. Tat hmat htar te` hnon phyit lo bar.
စိတ်မရှိပါနဲ့။ သတ်မှတ်ထားတဲ့ နှုန်းဖြစ်လို့ပါ။

Alright, please change for me the amount of .... American dollars.
Kaun Bi. Kyunaw`go American dollar .......... pho le`pay bar.
ကောင်းပြီ။ ကျွန်တော့်ကို အမေရိကန် ဒေါ်လာ .... ဖိုးလဲပေးပါ။

Alright.
Kaun Bi.
ကောင်းပြီ။

Numerals

Ga-nan Chey Myar:

ဂဏန်းခြေများ။

"What is your house number?"
"Khinbya ein nambat bae lauk lae?"
"The number is 35"
"Ein nambat thone sae nga bar"
"What is your phone number?"
"Khinbya telephone nambat be lauk lae?"
"My phone number is 417589."
"Kyunma telephone nambat ka lay tiq khun nga shit koe bar."

0	1	2	3	4	5	6	7	8	9
၀	၁	၂	၃	၄	၅	၆	၇	၈	၉

English Characters	Burmese Characters	Burmese Words	Pronunciation
1	၁	တစ်	Tit
2	၂	နှစ်	Hnit
3	၃	သုံး	Thone
4	၄	လေး	Lay
5	၅	ငါး	Ngar:
6	၆	ခြောက်	Chowk
7	၇	ခုနှစ်	Khon hnit
8	၈	ရှစ်	Shit
9	၉	ကိုး	Koe
10	၁၀	တစ်ဆယ်	Ta se`
11	၁၁	တစ်ဆယ့်တစ်	Ta seh tit
12	၁၂	တစ်ဆယ့်နှစ်	Ta seh hnit
13	၁၃	တဆယ့်သုံး	Seh thone
14	၁၄	တဆယ့်လေး	Seh lay
15	၁၅	တဆယ့်ငါး	Seh ngar
16	၁၆	တဆယ့်ခြောက်	Seh chowk
17	၁၇	တဆယ့်ခုန်	Seh khon
18	၁၈	တဆယ့်ရှစ်	Seh shit
19	၁၉	တဆယ့်ကိုး	Seh koe
20	၂၀	နှစ်ဆယ်	Hnit sei
21	၂၁	နှစ်ဆယ့် တစ်	Hnit seh tit
30	၃၀	သုံးဆယ်	Thone se`
40	၄၀	လေးဆယ်	Lay se`
50	၅၀	ငါးဆယ်	Ngar: se`
60	၆၀	ခြောက်ဆယ်	Chowk se`
70	၇၀	ခုနှစ်ဆယ်	Khon hnit se`
80	၈၀	ရှစ်ဆယ်	Shit se`
90	၉၀	ကိုးဆယ်	Koe se`
100	၁၀၀	တရာ	Ta yar
101	၁၀၁	တရာတစ်	Ta yah tit
110	၁၁၀	တရာ့တဆယ်	Ta yah ta seh

200	၂၀၀	နှစ်ရာ	*Hnit yar*
1,000	၁ ၀၀၀	တထောင်	*Ta htong*
10,000	၁၀ ၀၀၀	တသောင်း	*Ta thowng*
100,000	၁၀၀ ၀၀၀	တသိန်း	*Ta thein*
1,000,000	၁ ၀၀၀ ၀၀၀	တသန်း	*Ta than*

Ordinals
A-sin-pya-kain
အစဉ်ပြကိန်း။

First
Pahta ma
ပထမ

Second
Du.ti.ya
ဒုတိယ

Third
Ta' ti ya
တတိယ

Fourth
Zadou'hta
စတုတ္ထ

Fifth
Pyin sama
ပဉ္စမ

Sixth
Sa hta ma.
ဆဋ္ဌမ

Seventh
Tha ta ma
သတ္တမ

Eight
A'hta ma.
အဋ္ဌမ

Ninth
Nawama
နဝမ

Tenth
Da'tha ma.
ဒသမ

Useful Words And Phrases

Athone-win Thaw Zaga A-si-a-sin A-thone-a-hnone
အသုံးဝင်သော စကားအစီအစဉ်၊ အသုံးအနှုန်း။

How are you?
Maye`lar:/Nay Kaun: lar:?
မာရဲ့လား၊ နေကောင်းလား

I'm fine.
Mabaye`./Kaun: ba de`.
မာပါရဲ့။ ကောင်းပါတယ်။

Sir/Madam.
Khin bya:/Shin
ခင်ဗျား၊ ရှင်။

How do you do sir?
Maye`lar Khin bya:/Shin?
မာရဲ့လား ခင်ဗျား။ မာရဲ့လားရှင်။

I'm fine, sir.
Mabaye` khin bya:/Shin.
မာပါရဲ့ ခင်ဗျား၊ မာပါရဲ့ရှင်။

Please
Khin bya: (male speaker)/*Shin* (female)
ခင်ဗျား၊ ရှင်။

Excuse me.
Ga tawh bar ye`/Kwint Pyu Ba.
ကတော့ပါရဲ့၊ ခွင့်ပြုပါ။

Sorry
Seik mashi bar ne
စိတ်မရှိပါနဲ့။

Forgive me.
Kwint hlut par.
ခွင့်လွှတ်ပါ။

Thank you.
Kyei: zu: tin bar de`.
ကျေးဇူးတင်ပါတယ်။

Thank you very much.
Kyei: zu: amya: gyi tin bar de`.
ကျေးဇူးအများကြီးတင်ပါတယ်။

Don't mention.
Kek sa mashi bar bu:
ကိစ္စမရှိပါဘူး။

That's so/yes.
Houk ke`.
ဟုတ်ကဲ့။

That's not so/no.
Ma houk bu:
မဟုတ်ဘူး။

180

Do you understand?
Nar: le` da la:
နားလည်သလား။

I understand.
Nar: le` de`.
နားလည်တယ်။

I don't understand.
Nar: ma le bu:
နားမလည်ဘူး။

What?
Bar
ဘာ။

Say
Pyaw: da le`
ပြောသလဲ။

What (did you) say?
Bar pyo: da le`?
ဘာပြောသလဲ။

Slowly
Hnei` hnei`
နှေးနှေး။

Speak, please.
Pyaw: bar.
ပြောပါ။

Please speak slowly.
Hnei` hnei` pyaw: bar.
နေးနေးပြောပါ ။

Restaurant
Thamin zaing
ထမင်းဆိုင် ။

Where?
Bei hma le`?
ဘယ်မှာလဲ ။

Where's the restaurant?
Thamin zaing bei hma le`?
ထမင်းဆိုင်ဘယ်မှာလဲ ။

Hotel
Ho te`
ဟိုတယ် ။

Where's the hotel?
Ho te` bei hma le`?
ဟိုတယ်ဘယ်မှာလဲ ။

Train (railroad)
Miyatha
မီးရထား ။

Station
Budayon
ဘူတာရုံ ။

Where is the train (railroad) station?
Miyatha budayon bei hma le`?
မီးရထားဘူတာရဲ့ဘယ်မှာလဲ။

Toilet
Einda`.
အိမ်သာ။

Where is the toilet?
Einda bei hma le`?
အိမ်သာဘယ်မှာလဲ။

Is this taxi free?
Di te-ka-se ahh tha la
ဒီတက်စီအားသလား။

Vocabulary
Wal-har-ya-za-ga-lone Myar:
ဝေါဟာရစကားလုံးများ။

ambassador
than-amat
သံအမတ်

astrologer
bay-din-saya
ဗေဒင်ဆရာ

ant
paywe' seit
ပရွက်ဆိတ်

aunt
dawji/dawlay
ဒေါ်ကြီး။ ဒေါ်လေး

ashtray
sey-lake-pyar-chwet
ဆေးလိပ်ပြာခွက်

basket
chin-daung
ခြင်းထောင်း

bone
a-you:
အရိုး

be born
mwei(de)
မွေးတယ်

boxing
let-wheat-pwe
လက်ဝှေ့ပွဲ

beard
mou-seik-mwei
မုတ်ဆိတ်မွေး

bracelet
let kauk
လက်ကောက်

birthday
mwei-nay.
မွေးနေ့.

bridge
da.da
တံတား

184

body
kou-khanda
ကိုယ်ခန္ဓာ

buy
we (de)
ဝယ်တယ်

capital city
myodaw
မြို့တော်

close
peik-tae
ပိတ်တယ်

careful
tha-di-hta-dae
သတိထားတယ်

closer
na-mha
နားမှာ

cave
gu
ဂူ

copy
ku (de)
ကူးတယ်

child
kha-lay
ကလေး

culture
yin-kyey-mhu
ယဉ်ကျေးမှု

citizen
a'myo: tha/naingan tha
အမျိုးသား။ နိုင်ငံသား။

dance
ka'(de)
ကတယ်

divorce
kwa-shin-de
ကွာရှင်းတယ်

deposit
a'hta:(de)
အပ်ထားတယ်

doctor
sa-ya-won
ဆရာဝန်

die
sone-thwa-de
ဆုံးသွားတယ်

drive
maun-de
မောင်းတယ်

difficult
khet-de
ခက်တယ်

drums
sai-wai
ဆိုင်းဝိုင်း

embassy
than-yon:
သံရုံး

everyday
nay.-zin/nay.-dye
နေ့စဉ်॥ နေ့တိုင်း

family
mi-tha-zu
မိသားစု

fire
mie
မီး

festival
pwe-daw
ပွဲတော်

floor
a-htat
အထပ်

finger
lek-chaung
လက်ချောင်း

follow
lite-te
လိုက်တယ်

finish
pyi-de
ပြီးတယ်

genuine
asit-pyit-te
အစစ်ဖြစ်တယ်

guest
e`-the
ဧည့်သည်

186

grandchild
myei
မြေး

guide
lan-bya
လမ်းပြ

grandfather
aphoe
အဖိုး

hair
za'bin
ဆံပင်

hit
yaik-te
ရိုက်တယ်

happy
pyaw-de
ပျော်တယ်

holiday
a:-lat-yet
အားလပ်ရက်

help
ku-nyi-pay-bar
ကူညီပေးပါ

hospital
seyong
ဆေးရုံ

hire
hnga-de
ငှားတယ်

important
ayei-kyi-de
အရေးကြီးတယ်

iron
mie-bu
မီးပူ

insurance
arma-khan
အာမခံ

island
kyun
ကျွန်း

187

kickball
chin-lone
ခြင်းလုံး

knife
da
ဓါး

knee
du
ဒူး

late
naukya-de
နောက်ကျတယ်

like
kyaik-te
ကြိုက်တယ်

laugh
ye (de)
ရီတယ်

listen
na-htaung
နားထောင်

leather
tha-yay
သားရေ

love
chite
ချစ်တယ်

major
bouhmu
ဗိုလ်မှူး

mosque
bali
ဗလီ

many
a'-mya-gyi
အများကြီး

mosquito
chin
ခြင်

marry
mingala-saung-de
မင်္ဂလာဆောင်တယ်

mouth
ba-zat
ပါးစပ်

188

minister
won-gyi
ဝန်ကြီး

music
tha-chin-than
သီချင်းသံ

monkey
myauk
မျောက်

name
na-mae
နာမည်

newspaper
tha-din-za
သတင်းစာ

neighbourhood
won-kyin-dae-tha
ဝန်းကျင်ဒေသ

nurse
thu-nar-pyu
သူနာပြု

new
a-thit
အသစ်

ocean
pin-le
ပင်လယ်

open
phwin-te
ဖွင့်တယ်

only
tiq-khu-hte
တစ်ခုတည်း

paddy
za'ba:
စပါး

police
ye'
ရဲ

padlock
tho-ga-louk
သော့ခလောက်

pot
o`u
အိုး

parents
mi-ba
မိဘ

present
le'saung
လက်ဆောင်

parrot
kyetu-yqei
ကြက်တူရွေး

price
tan-phoo
တန်ဖိုး

pearl
pale`
ပုလဲ

quality
a-yi-a-thwe
အရည်အသွေး

raw
a-sein
အစိမ်း

rich
chan-tha-thaw
ချမ်းသာသော

refund
pyan-pay-de
ပြန်ပေးတယ်

rubber
kyet-paung-say
ကြက်ပေါင်စေး

remember
thadi-ya-de
သတိရတယ်

run
pyay-de
ပြေးတယ်

restaurant
sar-thauk-sai
စားသောက်ဆိုင်

schedule
pu-twe-par-sayin
ပူးတွဲပါစာရင်း

spoon
zun
ဇွန်း

seafood
pin-le-sar
ပင်လယ်စာ

stairs
hlei-ga
လှေခါး

sell
yaung-de
ရောင်းတယ်

station
bu-da-youn
ဘူတာရုံ

skin
a-thar-a-ye
အသားအရေ

storm
lay-mon-daing
လေမုန်တိုင်း

soft
nu-nyan-thaw
နူးညံ့သော

study
thin-kyar-de
သင်ကြားတယ်

tax
a-chun
အခွန်

ticket
let-mhat
လက်မှတ်

television
yoke-myin-than-kyar
ရုပ်မြင်သံကြား

toilet
ein-dha
အိမ်သာ

thick
a-htu
အထူ

tongue
sha
လျှာ

thief
thu-khoe
သူခိုး

touch
hti-de
ထိတယ်

thin
pain-par-thaw
ပိန်ပါးသော

typewriter
let-hnei-set
လက်နှိပ်စက်

thumb
let-ma
လက်မ

uncle
oo-lay/oo-gyi
ဦးလေး။ ဦးကြီး

upstairs
a-por-htat
အပေါ်ထပ်

understand
na-le-de
နားလည်တယ်

urinate
se-thwa-de
ဆီးသွားတယ်

vacant
lit-lat-te
လစ်လပ်တယ်

vegetable
hin-thi-hin-ywet
ဟင်းသီးဟင်းရွက်

walk
lan-shaute
လမ်းလျှောက်တယ်

water
yei
ရေ

wall
nan-yan
နံရံ

wife
za-nee
ဇနီး

wallet
pite-san-eight
ပိုက်ဆံအိတ်

zap
teik-kheik-thee
တိုက်ခိုက်သည်

zoo
ta-yeik-san-u-yin
တိရစ္ဆာန်ဥယျာဉ်

zebra
myin-gya
မျဉ်းကျား

zoology
thata-bay-da
သတ္တဗေဒ

zero
thonya
သုည

Bibliography

1. John Okell, (1971), *The Romanization of Burmese.*
2. Julian K. Wheatley, (1987), *Burmese Writing.*
3. Hasmat Bi@ Noreen Rashid, (2009), *English Borrowings in the Burmese Language.*
4. Pe Maung Tin and G. H. Luce (2008), *The Kings of Myanmar.*
5. *http://en.wikipedia.org/wiki/Burmese_language*
6. *http://www.myanmars.net/*
7. *http://www.seasite.niu.edu/burmese/Beginning/*
8. *http://www.guideformyanmar.com/*
9. *http://www.omniglot.com/writing/burmese.htm*

About the Author

Ma Tin Cho Mar is a language teacher in the University of Malaya and is currently involved in teaching and promoting Burmese language to undergraduates in the Faculty of Languages and Linguistics and also in the Faculty of Arts and Social Sciences.

She has actively participated in Literacy Campaigns during her years at the Yangon University and teaching Burmese language at camps. She was also a teacher in a Myanmar school.